Donna was born in 1967 during a heavy Communist Regime and graduated in Business Production. She completed an army training course for 2 years as part of the Regime policy. Donna had travelled around the world extensively, leaving the home country for the first time in 2000 to the Holy Land in Israel. In 2007 as a brave single mother, she arrived in the United Kingdom, learning through time to become fluent in 5 languages. In 2022, she published her first book.

I would like to dedicate this book to my family, which supported me in more than one ways to write this book. Also, to my older sister, who had important influence in my life. To my family members, who supported me in struggling time during these years. I would like to thank all of them.

Donna Ciuc

HUMAN DESIRE TOWARDS DETERMINATION

Adventures in Life

AUSTIN MACAULEY PUBLISHERS™
LONDON • CAMBRIDGE • NEW YORK • SHARJAH

Copyright © Donna Ciuc 2022

The right of Donna Ciuc to be identified as author of this work has been asserted by the author in accordance with section 77 and 78 of the Copyright, Designs and Patents Act 1988.

All rights reserved. No part of this publication may be reproduced, stored in a retrieval system, or transmitted in any form or by any means, electronic, mechanical, photocopying, recording, or otherwise, without the prior permission of the publishers.

Any person who commits any unauthorised act in relation to this publication may be liable to criminal prosecution and civil claims for damages.

All of the events in this memoir are true to the best of author's memory. The views expressed in this memoir are solely those of the author.

A CIP catalogue record for this title is available from the British Library.

ISBN 9781398424203 (Paperback)
ISBN 9781398424210 (ePub e-book)

www.austinmacauley.com

First Published 2022
Austin Macauley Publishers Ltd®
1 Canada Square
Canary Wharf
London

I am grateful and thankful to God, the Almighty, for his blessing throughout these years of protecting me, giving me the power to resolve any complications and protecting my life.

I am thankful to my family who have helped me through these years and in writing this book.

I would like to offer my special thanks to Austin Macauley Publishers who helped me publish this book to the world.

Steps from darkness, tours with angels, unknown goals and happiness, around the countries on your own.

Chapter 1

A beautiful little town where I was born is at the border with Ukraine, fascinating place with close mountains and rivers. Our house was at about 25-minute walk from the town centre where after the central part there was a large countryside with many trees, field, and farms. My mother got married at the age of 15 and my father at the age of 18 (in 1950s). They used to live with their grandparents, my mum had my older sister at the age of 17, then my other siblings were born. I was the last one born in my grandma's house. We all grew up in grandmother's house, Mother and Father used to work, and we took care of each other, brothers and sisters under Grandma's supervision. We adored Grandma as she, Grandpa, and my mum went through very difficult times in the Second World War. My mum was 5 when the Second World War started, and she remembered very well the Soviet occupation in the period 1944-1958. Grandpa used to be in the army during the war, when Russian army was passing, searching private houses for food provisions. I remember how Grandmother being on her own with the children in the house when the officers came to search, was terrified for her family's safety. She did not say anything to them as they took many sacks of wheat grains, corn grains, animals, and other goodies which the family had saved for winter times. As Soviets occupied the territories of Bessarabia, Northern Bukovina, Northern and Eastern Moldavia, all men were enrolled in the army and forced to fight for the Union to ensure they had free movement across these territories. The local civilians had obligation to provide a legal basis for the Soviet military presence in their territories. On the other side of the county was the German occupation taking place since 1941. Militaries from all these territories being allied under Soviet military ended their fight together to liberate the country from German occupation and they succeeded at the end of the year 1944. As a little child, I loved all history which my parents and grandparents experienced, they spent each evening with us around the fireplace to tell us various historical events and stories. I appreciated every single moment with them. When the Second World War was finished, people were very relieved and had back the freedom they deserved. Despite the struggles and still recovering from the war, people learned to appreciate every little thing in life and to be happy with it. I was always immensely proud of my grandad as he fought very bravely during those times. He taught us to appreciate everything in life and not to complain about unnecessary things.

I still remember when I was in year 1-2, my parents bought an old house. We moved in, it just had a kitchen and a very little room, Mum and Dad used to sleep in the kitchen—luckily, it was big enough to put a bed—whereas all of us 4 siblings were sleeping in the little room with one bed. The other part of the house was demolished, and we had started to build new one from scratch. You might say of me being so young and small, what do I know? I can assure you; I do remember how all works were going for about four years' length of time until we had proper house with few rooms. During this time, my little brother was born. My elder sisters and brothers being older, had the responsibilities to do work around the house and feed the animals which we had and took care of. My responsibility after school was to look after my little baby brother. Our generation grew up with responsibilities from noticeably young age. Being brought up by grandparents taught us to look after each other and all family members, because this is the way to keep happy and strong family.

Chapter 2

I was one of the five siblings born within a working-class family. I have always been a happy and bubbly child, also very tiny as I had been born premature, at 7 months, 1700g. I never liked eating food, thus I was growing very slow – a tiny little girl. During my childhood, I spent more time with the boys from my school than with the girls.

When I started school at 6 years old, I weighted 17 kg. Everyone laughed at me, shouting that my school bag looked bigger than me. Being so small, as you can imagine, led to various comments from my classmates. However, as tiny as I was, sitting in a first-row bench at school, I was happy of who I was and it never really bothered me. On the contrary, I have never taken any bullying. As tiny I was, I learned from a young age to always stand up for myself. I remember my mother always punished me because of the troubles happening at school, but my mother never knew that I was being bullied for my weight and height; everyone would laugh that I would be a dwarf, pygmy or midget.

For my parents and family, I was a normal little girl, loved the same as my other brothers and sisters. I was just enjoying my childhood as all children, and at school I was doing well. I was so happy to go to school, and my mom allowed me to walk alone to school as it was about 15 minutes from my childhood house.

One day in year 6, coming home from school, one of my classmates named Tony was pushing me out of the road on the way home and was laughing again at my little tiny figure.

"You little girl you need to go back to the year 2. You are a dwarf; we cannot see you because you are so small, and you are so not growing up. God must have forgotten about you," Tony laughingly shouted.

I asked politely to stop as this was not his first time, but he carried on.

I really felt that I should teach him a lesson to leave me alone, and I slowly approached to cross the bridge, grabbed his school bag with books and emptied it into the river.

"Now go home with your empty bag and stop bullying me." I was so confidently talking to him.

As expected on the next day, my mother was called by the school head teacher as Tony's parents complained. My mom came to school to see what had happened, and she was very upset with me. She took my books and gave them to Tony. I had to borrow books from other classmates or learn at school because Mom did not buy these books anymore. I still completed my 6th grade with good grades.

On another hand, after this incident, I was never bullied by anyone till the end of high school. My confidence was improving. I still had to face some situations where I had to fight for my rights. Since childhood, I learned to believe in myself, have confidence and understood that knowledge is my power.

Despite everything, I really enjoyed being at school, loved reading, outside activities. I really enjoyed exploring the geography knowledge about the other countries as I was born during the Communism period. I was really good at sports as well, such as running long distance, jumping from distance. I also attended a dance group which went around the country for different competitions. I always avoided complaining about daily life except the strict restrictions which we had to comply with from the communist regime. It was really, really annoying.

During the evenings, I would sit with a candle next to me to read because at 9 o'clock during the evening electricity was cut off. That was a real struggle for our nations.

During the school holidays, I wanted to go work. Being so tiny, it was very difficult to convince my parents to allow me to go to work somewhere. I started my first real job at the age of 13 in a farm where my dad was working, and I managed to beg him to take me for a trail. He took me one day, and I had to feed baby cattle. Feeding with bottle and looking after the baby cattle, I remember I was attracting a lot of attention as I myself was quite small and young.

"Whose child is here?" the workers asked, wondering.

"This is my daughter," my dad answered with pride.

"Why are you putting her to work from such a young age?" People were still in wonder.

"Well, her brother is already working in another department and she wanted to experience work as well. She was very keen on asking to be here!" my dad explained.

However, working hard to impress every worker there with my ability, I managed to convince them that I could help, and they were quite excited to have me there for a while. You could hear laughter in the farms so many times as people were joyful and working together. My dad used to take me in the morning at 6 a.m. and we would come back at 6 o'clock in the evening for two consecutive months during the entire school holiday. This was my first work as a young child completing such long hours, with limited lunch break.

Each school holiday, I liked working there and earning spare money for myself which I was saving before the school starts, learning to be independent as much as I could. I always had support from my parents and older sister; however, I wanted to be independent and was also interested in different jobs which I could do in the farm. I also did some work afterwards for the fruits conservation factory, coffee shop and different jobs where I could gain experience and understand the work in various departments.

Every second evening, I would spend reading books and studying for school. Only the electricity cutting in the evening was restricting me, and I was not able to read as much as I wished for. As a child, I was hoping that this will change one day. My mom was always asking me to go to sleep, and I would beg her to allow me to read one hour more.

After several years passed, I started studying at the local college in the city which opened my eyes even more living independently and travelling across the country. During my college years, I joined pre-army training, which was one of my big dreams, as I was growing taller and had the opportunity to challenge myself. I was so happy when I was accepted in the group, predominantly formed by young boys with only two girls.

I remember the first uniform for training was royal blue colour army uniform. Joining the training, I got a more muscular body and felt like I was growing taller day by day. If all my primary school classmates could see me now, they would be so surprised – especially me joining the special forces! Training was tough; in five minutes, I had to dress, make the bed, tidy myself and be outside for report to command. Good organisational skills and exceptional timing skills was crucial. If someone was late for report, they would be given a punishment to run several times around the camp, sometimes, even further to clean all the barracks during the whole day. Many of my colleagues dropped out of the training after couple of weeks. However, I was enjoying the tough training, knowing that it would help me to go through life and become very independent.

Uniforms had to always be clean, boots to shine – this is called discipline which you learn obligatory of you get punished. During the training, I really enjoyed the different activities and especially when we went out in the forest for shooting and learning to clean every component of different weapons, small pistols to Kalashnikov 45. As a girl, you would have needed to be mentally strong to comply with all these rules and integrate in a group where majority of the trainees were men.

After few months, I was recognised for best time-keeping skills and learning path of army in a field with grade of command. It was one of the unique feelings, I felt proud of my achievement.

During the '80s' time, the army for men was still compulsory as everyone needed to be trained for war. Communist era was keeping us under control. Training was very formal; learning patterns were very confidential. I was very proud that I was in this training. It also gave me the opportunity to learn the importance of punctuality, body language, send message straightforward to subject, to be mentally strong and much more. These two years of training gave me a lot of confidence about myself.

Despite all restrictions, I liked learning about everything. I even became member of a syndicate organisation since college, joining different meeting regarding our communism regime. We had to respect this regime otherwise would be questioned if you would have anything against the regime.

My favourite subjects at college were mathematics, physics and chemistry. My teacher was pushing me to pursue further education in the mathematics gymnasium as I graduated in Maths with A*. Teachers called my parents from the college and asked them to convince me to go for Mathematics University because the country was needing mathematics teachers; however, I set up my mind already. I was interested more in high-profile army academy, although my parents said that academy is for boys not girls and did not allow me to go. I switched to business management course at the other side of the country. It was the best time for my young later-teenage years, quite easy to get through as I had high grades every year. I finished and returned back home, got a job straightaway after qualification as it was no problem to get job at those time with high grades.

My first really good job was in import-export management with good money and colleagues respect. However, it was not my dream job. I always wanted to work in top army to find out why communism regime restricted our nation to the severe extent. Daily life for some people was very hard as all the basic food supplies were limited; people were queuing for hours in a shop to get first aid help as well. Big inequality during these times always bothered me, although we were lucky as our family had better supplies from other relatives. The country was rich; however; our communist dictator was sending neighbours all food supplies for trade but by the cause of starving his own country, his own nation. I remember at one of the syndicate meetings, I asked couple of questions about the country's overall wellbeing and the population's needs. After this, I felt I was being watched closely for a long time and had to participate in many additional meetings which my company required, making sure I do not have negative influence on the communist regime. I always stood up for the working-class society as being my own society, and moreover, the working class sustains a country.

One sunny afternoon, my mother was baking bread – the smell of freshly baked bread was irresistible – one gypsy woman came to my mom, begged a bread in exchange to tell my mother her daughter's future. Growing up in an Orthodox Christian family, I could not really take it serious and listen to this prediction; however, Mom gave her a piece of bread by saying that we need to give bread to a hungry person, and the gypsy asked me to show her my palm.

"What is your name, bubbly girl?" she asked smiling.

"Dora," I replied.

"Aw, poor young girl, you are so jolly and bubbly, but if you know what you will have to go through in your life, you will not believe," she said with a scary voice.

"Ha ha, you think I will believe your lies?" I laughed.

My mother was listening without saying a word. Then the gypsy woman said:

"Dora, Dora! You will get married in couple of years, and it will not last long. You will have everything material, lovely house, good job; but one day, you will leave everything behind and will travel over the seas. You will be not happy! Before that, you will have two car accidents during one-year time, but you will be saved. Your life will be very difficult, but you will succeed with ups and downs. You will get over everything which will be not an easy life. All this journey will be in your own hands."

"Ha ha, thank you for your lies, madam gypsy; you earn your bread now," I replied.

I had gone out with my friends, telling them what a prediction I had and made them laugh at that. My mother was a bit concerned about this as she said that some of the gypsies can predict your future to some extent. Never believed a word what she told me. I was always making jokes about that until the day came and many of the situations she mentioned happened. I have gone through the accidents during my late teenage times. I was slightly scared as it happened so fast, and I remembered straightaway the gypsy woman's words. In one year, I have been hit twice by car. Thanks to God, they were not major accidents. I still was making jokes about my prediction, still had doubted that it could have a slight truth about my life. I continued with my life. Whatever was in front of me, nothing was stopping me from enjoying the life with friends and family.

One evening, I came from work, spoke with my mom about how my day was and said that I was going to sleep as I was feeling tired and it was a bit late. After couple of hours, I woke up at 2 a.m. to go to the bathroom. I tried to turn on the lights, but as usual, it was cut down as communism regime was strict on hours. I fainted by the door in my bedroom. Luckily, my mother heard the noise from her bedroom and came to see me. My parents were so terrified, seeing me at the floor with no breath or movement. They tried to awaken me, but I was not responding. They called my sister who was living few houses down the road. She called the ambulance; however, when the ambulance arrived, the doctor said that I was in clinical death and not much could be done now.

Three hours later, at 5 a.m., when the ambulance was still in, I woke up and asked:

"What has happened? Why all these candles are around me?"

Seeing their face expression, my mother replied, "We ask you what happened because you were not breathing for three hours!"

I laughed and replied, "I had beautiful dream and went up with angels for a while."

"What are you talking about?" my mother asked, confused.

"Yes, I had two angels with me who just brought me back."

Everyone was looking at me like I was an alien... I came back from clinical death... I was taken to hospital for investigation, two days continually went under medical investigation and discharged without any diagnosis or symptoms and no explanation to what could have happened to me.

Let me walk you through my beautiful dream:

Two heavenly angels came down and took me to the unknown place far up in a very peaceful environment. These white bright angels lifted me from my bed by taking me each by my arms and took me with them to this place to which probably not many of us believe that exists. I, a strong-minded grown woman, who went through many experiences in my life, can confirm to you that it does exist. I have been there, have seen its so peaceful entrance to the unknown place.

While the angels walked me, they showed me 12 grey gothic doors, and they explained to me who will go through every single door as we will not get in through the same door, all of us. The 12th door was slightly open. I asked if I could go in to see how it looks inside. One of the angels said with a very clear voice:

"No, you cannot go in, for whoever is going in through to any of these doors is not coming back, and your time is not yet to go. You must go back because you have to do many things in your life. You did not finish your transit on earth. Say to people what you have seen, and enjoy your life."

After this was said, the angels brought me back down and I woke up.

Many of you will think this was just a dream. No, when you dream, you are alive. I was in clinical death and came back; this is the big difference. However, you believe or not, your soul will still go to this beautiful place according to your deeds on earth.

I was brought up in this communism regime where I had to work Sundays just to prevent people to socialise in public places. However, this did not stop me from visiting many monasteries and exploring Christianity. I believed in God since a small child. Believing in God, I had no fear of people. I walked at nights on the streets to go to work though the side of dark roads but never feared anything.

From childhood, I was always interested in different cultures, religions and Israel as Holy Land. I have read quite a lot about it as in late 1960–1998 under the communist regime, there were many restrictions. But still managed to visit few countries during the communism with my sister with short visa periods. We also saw how the life in other countries was going, under the socialism regime. In Russia, there was also communism but the lifestyle was a lot better than in our country. As times were going and passing by, I was dreaming that one day, I will get to see the Holy Land.

In early 20s, I decided to marry Ray with big wedding and ceremony. However, he was not the right person, and as a young girl, I made this mistake thinking that this person will change with time. My mother tried to tell me that this is not the right person for me because Ray embraced drinking life. One thing I regret was that I did not listen my mother at this time and rushed to get married. On the engagement day, Ray was partying all day with his ex-girlfriend and came at our house, very late in the evening. We were newly engaged; that seemed so wrong, I see this now, but could not see it then. I did not take my mother's advice; I got married and wasted big wedding ceremony for reputation.

After a year, we bought massive house. We had good holidays. Everything was going very good financially as we both had good jobs. During the communism, we had to prove from where we had money for everything as we were very young. We had all paperwork to prove, and it was not an issue. Whoever lived during communist regime probably knows how life was. In the following years, we had small farm with pigs, cows, turkeys, goose, ducks and a dozen chickens. As you can imagine, we did not lack anything, from food or money plus good jobs. House was built beautifully with an extension, two kitchens – one for the summer days, one was winter kitchen – plus few rooms lovely decorated and furnished. That takes a few years, then just live beautiful life.

One element was missing, which is the most important, happiness!!! Trying to stop Ray from heavy drinking habits, trying everything possible, left me over time with no other choices. Every time when we had a discussion about his drinking problem, he would promise me that he would not drink so much anymore. However, that lasted one or two days. As a young woman, I was still thinking once we have family, children, maybe he will change.

One sunny winter afternoon, I felt pregnant, and I hoped for changes and that we would build a beautiful family. After few months, I gave birth to my beautiful boy Daren. Surprisingly, when I give birth, instead having my husband next to me, he did not visit me in a hospital for three days. I sent my relatives to check on him because I was worried about him.

After few days, I was discharged and came home. I was still hoping for him to change his drinking habit. My baby was not very good at sleeping nights at all, few minutes then awake. I did not have opportunity to rest at all; had my family member helping me sometimes. One evening on a winter day, being exhausted, I asked my husband Ray:

"Ray, would you like to stay with the baby for couple of hours from 8 p.m. to 10 p.m.? Then I can rest a bit because I am exhausted."

"NO! You are staying at home every day, but I am working tomorrow at 7 a.m.," he replied.

Well, that was an answer straight to my heart; however, I carried on to do my job as a new mother, looking after my baby. Never had help from him as a normal family which helps each other in needs. Many nights, I did not switch off the light in the room as baby was not sleeping more than few minutes at the time.

After one and a half month, Daren got high temperature, and we were admitted to hospital on emergency issue. As we arrived, the baby was taken away from me as he was struggling with breathing, and I was left outside the emergency room, where the doctor took the baby. It was a very scary moment for a mother. It was the longest time of my life to wait on my own under the doctor's door waiting for an answer from Doctor. Baby was really taken good care of by the doctors who managed to bring him to a healthy life. It was again tough times that the baby was not sleeping at nights or days more than an hour maximum, and I was alone again with everything. When you are a couple, then you expect to share all work as a couple, but this was not the case in my situation. I did not give up. I was really struggling but I kept smiling and keeping up with everything.

Time was going on. At seven months of maternity, I was called back to work as business was very busy. I had two options: going back to work or losing my job. I held a good job so decided to find a good nanny and return to work as my little boy also started sleeping better at nights. I had finally found a good nanny and returned to work.

The child was growing; however, his dad was not changing from his drinking habit. One day, I asked him about some rumours which were going around about him at work. Then I was slapped by him so badly that I passed out and woke up on the floor with black eyes and blood on my face and around me. He left me on the floor and went to drink in a pub because I asked a question about other women which he visited at work (Remember: Smoke does not come out without fire). There was a truth about it; I did not expect that he would punch me so quickly. After this incident, I explained that I will not take this behaviour any longer from him and there will be consequences. Other times when he was drunk, he was abusive even to his little son Daren.

Life was continuing, and materially, there seemed to be no problem; everything was working out for us professionally, and I had the most beautiful house and garden. However, my soul was always in pain as I happened to realise my marriage might have not been the right turn for me. I had been suffering in silence for years and years, trying to avoid showing my pain to anyone. It is not a cliché; everything which society thinks brings you value or happiness, I had it all and was so unhappy. I was living in an abusive environment with some domestic violence, a child who was petrified of his dad, who when coming home from work drunk would abuse him and myself. As many young women in this situation, I was ashamed to confess this to other neighbours or anyone in the family.

Having a partner with alcohol problem, I could never rely on him. Once back in these terrifying times, he nearly burned the house being drunk. In short, he left the electrical cooker on the top cupboard in the kitchen, fell asleep, and half of the furniture in the kitchen got on fire. Quite luckily, neighbours saw this and called the fire brigade, saving the house as I was at work. All these years, I had accumulated silently the anger, unhappiness and worries about my son who was at this early age in an inappropriate environment for a small child. Thus, one courageous day when me and my son was physically abused, I decided that the time had come to take action to get out of this mess.

It was a bank holiday. I was waiting for my friends to come to visit me. However, my husband again was drunk already, instead of helping me and enjoying together this special day. I cooked quite a lot of food just to enjoy, but when I saw my husband walking half-drunk and verbally abusing again, it ruined the happy mood. My friends asked me how do I manage to deal with him? I smiled and said that I have to manage; end of the day he is my husband. After my friends left, he was already very drunk and wanted to take my child to the city centre with him for a walk. My son started to scream that he was not going with his dad anywhere. How surprising that a child at the age of four already understood that his dad was drunk and could feel uncomfortable with him. I had to calm the situation, explaining to my husband that it was already late and the child cannot go anywhere. It was not so simple to deal with a drunk husband and small child. Also, for the sake of safety, I would have never allowed my child to go with him being drunk; however, I had to find the right approach to explain this.

Unfortunately, that was my daily life. How much of happiness I could have had? In the meantime, I was thinking what would be the best way to get out from this unhappy marriage. Materially satisfied, nobody was really going to understand that you are having everything but you are not happy. I didn't want to spend all my life in an unhappy marriage, verbally and physically abused and, most importantly, my child being traumatised seeing his own father drunk.

Coming from work one evening, my poor son was with all dirty clothing on, sleeping and crying in sleep. When he felt my touch, he jumped to my neck, hugged me and said: "Mammy, Mammy, Daddy had beaten me because I broke by mistake one branch from the apple tree in the garden."

I was shocked by my child's distress, and after I saw on his little legs how his dad left marks from beating him, I was so furious. His dad was quietly sleeping being drunk with no worries and cares about his own child. The next day, I told him firmly that this was unacceptable behaviour from father to child.

"I was drunk!" he replied.

"This is not an acceptable excuse," I told him. "You need to stop drinking, otherwise you will lose us."

"Ha ha, I will not stop drinking because of you; where you would go? I am not going out from the house, and you do not have anywhere to go!" he replied.

"My dear, you will remain one day with your house and your drink all alone, and we will leave you!" I assured him. I added further, "Never be so sure. You have in your hands: family or drinking. Decide before it is too late!"

"Ha ha, will see where you will go. At the end of the day, you love this house," he replied.

"I beg you, take our conversation seriously as you are sober now, and hear what I have told you," I added.

This was the time I had to take a decision for my life and my child's future, in a gentle and clever way to manage to get out of this house. At my workplace, there was an opportunity of redundancy, so I applied for the redundancy provision and I was approved, claiming this to be the best option for a mother with a child. The plan was put in place already. I had to find where I could leave my son in a safe place. My sister agreed to look after my son which was a big relief for me, knowing that he will be looked after.

I researched which country was offering jobs abroad. Smoothly, I managed to find an agency where I could apply for a job abroad, applying straightaway for three countries, Israel, Greece and Italy, for work visa. I proceeded with my paperwork, and after two months, I received the visa for Israel. I felt that God brought my dream to reality. I managed, in the meantime, to arrange with my sister to take care of my son Daron, so that he could have the best care and we would manage to move out from our stressful house. I knew it would be a very hard movement to do; however, I put in risk everything for my son's safety and my escape from this heavy-drinking husband.

Chapter 3

When I got the visa for Israel, my family members were worried slightly about me as I was going so far away on my own during the time of big conflicts in Israel. I was happy that I could get out of my unhappy marriage. With a broken heart, leaving my little boy Daron behind, I got on the flight to Israel for work, with my mind settled to offer the best for my child. On my own with faith in God, I was not looking back for a second. God gave me the chance to go, and I am grateful for it, and I was ready to embrace with all my heart this opportunity.

When I stepped out from the airport, I realised part of the saying from this gypsy woman is becoming true. I started to believe that the things about my life were coming together, started to believe that what she said was coming into reality. Walking out from airport in Tel Aviv with the lady from the agency, I was feeling as I was flying in the air because I was in the Holy Land. My satisfaction to step on this land made me stop, touch with my hand the land, then give thanks to God for this blessing.

My instruction from the agency was that I would be a carer for an elderly lady. Surprisingly, when I arrived to the agency in Israel, it turned to be a totally different story; there was a family which I would have to take care of and an elderly gentleman with disability. Well, for me personally, it was not important as I do take full responsibility once I receive a job. Also, I had paid the commission of $3,000 to the agency. There was no other way, as I had a loan for the money I paid, I had to accept the job no matter what conditions were offered. The issues I have experienced were mainly due to language barrier because speaking Slavic languages, I was contracted to work with a Polish-speaking person; however, the actual person I taking care of was speaking just Yiddish and Hebrew. Thus, his wife had to translate between me and her husband, which for a carer could be very complicated work. With not many options, I had to adapt and comply with all rules and work environment.

Every single evening, my pillow was wet from my tears not stopping as I knew my son was so far from me, and we did not have access to communicate often. It was really challenging financial times as I was saving every penny to send for my son and pay the loan. Crying, I had to remain calm, and I started learning Hebrew every single minute available. Teaching myself from books, dictionary, listening to other people, listening to TV programs in Hebrew, I was able to learn the basic communication after three months. In these three months, I had not slept one night in peace. I lost 20 kg in the span of three months; however, I had set a goal that I would die or be alive but would not give up my work for anything in the world. To be a carer means often 24 hours from 24 hours a day. Whoever has worked as a carer internally probably would agree.

After I started to understand the language, I had 12 hours off given in the week for rest, and I found a cleaning job during this free time from a family to earn extra money for myself. In the meanwhile, determination for future was making me stronger. The people I worked for were happy with me. I was doing everything what was required from my job, and often I was exceeding at my duties, with hope that one day I would fully repay my loan and get earnings for myself and my son. Day by day, I was becoming better at Hebrew language and understanding the culture, which made it easier to communicate with my employer. My employer's family was coming around and sometimes were helping me.

As I started spending more time with this family, speaking with one very gentle elderly lady one evening, she told me how she arrived after the Second World War and how being taken with her parents and brother to German lagers, their life was miserable and persecuted by Germans under Hitler's command. She was the only one from the entire family to be able to make this journey from Poland back to Palestine. When she arrived, she was put in a shared marquee; she was just a child when this event happened. I just saw the other side, and to go through this was heart breaking. She was, on the contrary, so thankful that she made it alive to Israel. To hear this story, you understand why they have nightmares at night, and they are waking up constantly as this trauma is living with her for life. These stories, which younger generation could not understand, speaking with this lady made my heart melt and I had forgotten all the moments whenever she was harsh with me sometimes. I was able to understand, from the other side, the behaviour of a person who had gone through so much. I always gave respect to these people.

The days were passing by, and I was taking my employer in a wheelchair to the synagogue every Saturday (Shabbat). I started to communicate with people and was getting out from the house. Having access to call my son and family back home was helping me to adapt easier in the place. Sunday, 6 May 2001, was my first trip to Jerusalem to the Holy Place, and I had just realised that my dream was becoming a reality to see the old city of Jerusalem. It was a more than interesting city which is shared by three religions: Christians, Jews and Muslims. Beautiful old city which contains more than 1,700 years of experience. This is the city where Christians Pilgrimage was come to visit for more than 1000 years to discover Christianity. They used ships for travelling on the sea, compared to nowadays travelling by plane. To discover Christianity, they were traveling for weeks and months.

I was walking in the Holy site, Via Dolorosa (translated often: The Way of Suffering) route where Jesus walked on the way to His crucifixion. There were 14 stations to the place where Jesus is laid in the tomb. I always believed in the Holy Book, The Bible, but the feeling of walking the same route where Jesus walked was very emotional and extraordinary for me. Stepping in the Church of the Holy Sepulchre, Temple Mount identified as place of crucifixion and tomb of Jesus of Nazareth, I was feeling emotional; my feet got weaker, my hand started shaking as I approached to the stone where Jesus' body was prepared for burial, called stone of Anointing. There was an aroma from the stone of Holy Essence. When I touched the stone, I felt that my soul is free, clean and happy to be in this place. I was praying and giving thanks to God for His help to get to the place I have always dreamed since childhood. Many people around, from all over the world, were sharing the same interest as me as taking stairs up to the chapel which is built on the rock of Calvary (the 12th station of the cross) Golgotha. Every moment was very special. I was sitting and feeling the peace within my soul and the Holy Spirit, standing with a candle in the hand in this chapel, praying for family, friends and all people who were in need.

After a while, walking down, I went to the Chapel where Jesus had been laid in a tomb and from which He rose again. Many people were queuing to get in. Standing in the queue, I had time to admire the place, feeling the emotion was growing as I was getting closer. When I walked in the Chapel with the other three visitors, I felt so relieved, clean soul, clean mind, could not think for anything from outside except feeling of peace, unity in the community of Christian faith.

With a peace within my soul, I left the place and returned to work. Happy and fulfilled with my experience today was something that I knew I would remember forever. This special moment I cannot forget as I have never felt this emotion before in my entire life.

Coming back home from my day off with some food from my friend, happy that I saw the Holy place, my happiness suddenly was disturbed as I was told off to go outside in the balcony to eat my food with plastic cutlery. Being in their house and understanding their culture, I did not hesitate a minute. I grabbed the plastic cutlery, complied like a good child, and I went on the balcony with my food and plastic cutlery and ate all alone in the cold with tears rolling down on my face.

With all requirements, nothing stopped me from my determination of being a good, hardworking mother and dream for my freedom in the future. Earning $600 a month, I was paying $500 for my loan for six months; the rest $100 and money from cleaning on my day off, I was sending to my sister for my son. This amount of money was earned with many tears; however, I appreciated every single penny, knowing that one day, I would finish to repay my loan.

Chapter 4

The first month when I started to enjoy my salary, I was thinking that I need to start to save to buy a roof over my son's head. I did not think of my own needs first. As a mother, everything was for my little boy to make sure I will be able to bring him up with my sister's help (God bless her) and offer him a roof over his head. I wanted also to help him for further education; this was my goal for the following years ahead.

As time was passing, my employer got really ill and was admitted in hospital. I was going every single day to stay in the hospital with him, and when I was leaving, he always said, "Please do not leave me alone; stay with me." It was a hospital and he was not alone, but that connection as being 24/7 was hard for him there which is understandable. When I came home in the evening, I was cooking and cleaning everything as his wife was at home, and I had to help her as well.

One Sunday, I had a day off from work, and I was really in a happy mood in the morning. I got myself ready to travel to Tel Aviv's seaside in order to meet some friends whom I met while working for my employers. With so much excitement, I caught the minibus to Tel Aviv, then walked along Allenby road towards the seaside in front of Carmel Market as the pavement was cordoned by police because there was a suspicion of a subway bomb. I was so in a hurry to get to the sea that instead of waiting until the access to the road was open, I just walked in between the cars in the middle of the road to the other side of the road where my friend was, without even thinking of the consequences. As I walked down, the police officer ran and shouted after me, but I had already crossed to other side. I felt embarrassed afterwards as I had been told that if in a circumstance there was an exploding bomb during me crossing, I would have put both myself and the police officer who run after me in danger. One of the friends who was there, remained speechless when she saw me. I just carried on like nothing had happened. Israel is a Holy Land but there never has been peace. I enjoyed my first day on the seaside after nearly a year in Israel.

After couple of months in the hospital, my employer passed away. That was hard for me as I got used to being his personal carer. Now I did not even know what would be happening to my job. After family discussion, they decided that it would be good if I would like to stay with their mom but with condition that I accept a salary cut and six hours daily taking off. With not many options, I had to accept the offer and see how things would work out. Slowly, I started taking care of his wife; however, due to the salary cut and the six hours off every day from 14:00 to 20:00, I had to figure out quickly for additional income. I found some jobs in cleaning. I was happy with this, but unfortunately, I developed an allergy from the cleaning chemical products which I used, and it turned into a real struggle for me to be working in this industry. I still tried to work, tried to find something else, but it was not so easy. I asked my agency for a different full-time internal job but there was also no luck. I kept trying to work in between my free hours; however, my allergy got worse off and I could not continue.

Chapter 5

Coming from work, I wanted to meet my friends for a chat in Rishon LeZion Park where I used to go with my previous employer. We were meeting his friends there for years and years. We used to play games and learn about each other's life history as most of the people were from over the world, settled in Israel after Second World War. This was an incredibly beautiful place, after work for relaxation. It also had a little lake and lovely birds. Always there were many people during the day and especially during the late afternoon.

I met few friends, Ora, Natalie, Cristina for couple of hours, then I left to go home. As I arrived at my house (which was not far from the park, called Nahalat), I just put the key in to open my door, and suddenly, I heard a massive explosion from not far away.

BOOM!!! (11:03 p.m.)

O My God! My heart started beating, and I started to worry about my friends who I left behind. I tried to call them, but there was no signal. As usual, after an explosion, signal automatically starts failing. I locked the door and went back to the park to check on my friends. It was my first shock to see what was going on. I felt such pain of a family losing their friends and family members. The whole park was barricaded by police and ambulances; services were very quick for this situation. It was so scary real-life situation of blood and injured bodies everywhere on the playing area. I looked for my friends, and luckily, I met two of them who were also very worried about the others. I was so upset and angry that all of those innocent people, old, young, Israeli, foreigners, died there while just relaxing and enjoying their time in a park. It was a suicide bombing which took 15 innocent lives and 57 injured. It was a handmade bomb; screws, metal were all over the area. First incident I saw live was on the TV; however, to see this in reality, it really shook me. I was also angry that some people would not respect life and take innocents life – life which passed the Second World War, crossed the world to come to Israel had been taken away spending their retirement time in the park with friends. I found this to be very cruel. Animals who in nature are killing another animal to survive for food is something which I understand in nature; however, to kill just because people are not from the same religion or nationality is incomprehensible to me. Another learning curve to understand humanity and value for people.

I walked home with friends with a broken heart about the situation; however, we had to continue our life and go ahead. After couple of days, we met again in the same place in the park. We lit candles and paid tribute to the people who lost their lives there. The place was beautiful, so people were coming there, and we kept meeting in the same park after what has happened. Knowing the risk which was there, we were keeping our faith and determination to help us overcome the fear and continue living normally.

After work, I was still meeting friends on the seaside in Tel Aviv, enjoying every single minute possible in this beautiful country. The old city Yafo was one of the oldest parts of the Tel Aviv, also the city where I was going to the church on Sundays to meet people from everywhere from the world as Israel has an incredible history and people were coming to visit. Also, Yafo was known to be the first port for Israel to trade with other countries hundreds of years ago and is still the oldest port in history.

In Jaffa, there were many museums with well-known artists. This city-village was a combination of old and modern architectures. It was a beautiful multi-ethnic place, Jews, Muslims and Christians living together. Some of the streets were in a very old authentic style with small open markets where you could find variety of cultural stocks and people from wherever. Walking from the church, I admired the old buildings of churches, mosques and synagogues alongside the Jaffa Port. From one side, old authentic streets, from another, new buildings creating a mixture of life in the community. Children were often playing together outside the port, which always has proven to myself that children do not have such fake walls created by the adults in terms of nationality and religious aspirations, so we as adults would need to take the example from them to live in peace and harmony.

As I was walking down the Jaffa promenade, it really amazed me, all of the restaurants which were selling their services in three different languages alongside with fresh fish from the sea. The air was so fresh with light breeze from the sea, making me feel that was the best time I could have to relax in the middle of this beautiful place. I had always been advised by my friends that Jaffa sells the best humus, so I decided to have a lunch and try their speciality in one of the restaurants by the seaside. I ordered humus and three different types of fresh fish. I must admit this was such a lovely meal accompanied with the fresh air from the sea.

After this lovely meal and delicious ice cream, I walked ten minutes to Tel Aviv seaside. Sunday late afternoon, I could not believe how many people were coming by the seaside after work. Beach was full of people, children and all nationalities sharing beautiful place in the sun – white sand beach with long promenade. I also found out that every evening during the summer or autumn, there are activities on the beach, welcoming everyone to join. That Sunday, as I was passing by a dancing club, there was all type of music and everyone was dancing; people interacted with each other and socialised. I could see the happiness on the people's face and their joy in the eyes.

Tel Aviv is also multi-ethnic city, quite modern with a lot of tourists and holidaymakers. Walking down the Allenby street, I stopped in a Carmel Market, another multi-culture city with a unique market with old and authentic to newly fashioned style goods for everyone. Down the road, you start to see all of the tall glass buildings; this was the business area, a very modern part of the city of Tel Aviv. As I was passing by, I saw many museums along the Dizengoff road, beautiful city and within a walking distance. On the way back to work, I decided to try another Israeli food, shawarma, one of the famous street foods. It was yummy, with a delicious freshly made salad. I really spoiled myself today with these goodies in this beautiful city.

I remember during my city walk, I saw many soldiers with guns; however, this is normal for our safety to see army around. This showed the security and protection in this country. Massive supermarkets ahead, on the entrance security guard welcomed me. Sunday evening about 7 p.m. all the shops were open, and every shop warmly welcomed me to the shop; friendly feeling attracts people to the shop. I spent an amazing day, learned so much from my own experience and was very happy I could experience these beautiful things.

This city never sleeps. Day or night, there were people around. People here were genuinely very friendly, chatty which makes everyone welcome despite race, religion, colour, etc. I made many friends from different countries, Israel, India, Canada, Italy, Australia, Moldavia, Philippine, and we are still until today good friends and in touch with each other. Life is beautiful on its own, despite all hardships, if your mind is always with good thoughts for yourself and others. Whatever happens, take it as an experience, learn from it; live your life and respect people, and you will be respected.

Chapter 6

The Tel Aviv central bus station, Tahana Merkazit, is a place where majority foreign workers would meet up for a drink and shopping. The place was full of people enjoying their day off and meeting their friends – happy atmosphere. After a chat with my friends, I decided to leave to go for shopping, while another of my very dear friend said that she would come with me as she needed to do some shopping. As we were walking out of the station, maybe 100 metres toward the city, there was a massive explosion behind. Suicide bombing took place there where we had been minutes ago drinking with friends (5 January 2003). We rushed back to the place. It was unrecognisable, blood everywhere, injured people lying on the floor, another shock scene in reality. In five minutes, police and ambulances came over. They were very good and prompt in this situation. It is so difficult to understand people who could take such a cruel action for no reason. Innocent people who are working hard to provide necessity for their families, everybody with different reasons coming to work together. Another shocking experience happened in a place where any of us could have been, another 23 innocent people lost their lives. (15 Israeli plus 8 foreigners).

Again, after a while, life was going ahead, day by day; nothing could make me to change my mind, my strong belief that God is with me and He is protecting me. All what I saw and experienced day by day was teaching me to value everything I had, to believe in myself and respect everyone around me.

One day, during my time off, I decided to treat myself to go and have my hair done in a beauty salon. I asked the lady if she could complete full cut, colour and highlights. During the colouring process, I was OK; however, after the lady put the mixture for the highlights, something went really wrong. Professionals should know the basic rules that it is not recommended to mixed hair colours from two different brands as all colours contain different chemicals and some chemicals would not be suitable combined together. When she put on my hair the second colour, I felt that my scalp was burning. I asked few times to be washed as I was feeling that my skin was burning, but she was understaffed and quite busy, and couple of times ignored me until I said I am going myself to wash because I feel my forehead started swelling already. In a few minutes, she washed my hair and I left the shop.

Going home, I felt my forehead was getting bigger and bigger. After couple of hours, I realised that I had gotten a severe allergy which was progressing very quickly. Urgently, I found a private doctor to see me. He gave me medication assuring by morning I would be okay. Unfortunately, it did not happen; by the morning, my head was having an enormous shape, and my eyes were completely swollen that I could not even see at all. Everyone went to work. I remained by myself indoors, could not call or answer my phone as I was not able to see. I tried to feel the phone buttons to answer, however unsuccessful attempt. For my luck, my friend Rivka got worried about me that I did not answer her calls and she knew from evening that I developed the allergy, so she just came in with Bertha to see me, as she felt something was not right. When they arrived, they were so shocked to see me staying in my room helpless in this state. Rivka said:

"Dora, we need to take you to the emergency ASAP!!! Your head has tripled in size and you are blind because your eyes are very swollen."

"Yes, please Rivka. I feel I cannot breathe properly as well."

Bertha dressed me; then they walked me to the car, urgently driving to Emergency. Like in a dream, I heard about 20 doctors saying:

"Let's try to save her life first; she has about 10–15 minutes then her airway will be completely blocked."

The doctors gave me injections of prednisone, and the other doctors were saying:

"Let's try to see if we can save her eyes, her vision, otherwise she will remain blind."

Nothing ever was scarier than this experience. I am quite a strong person; I do not give up, have gone through many things already, but this one is the worst experience I have ever had. I stayed in hospital, and after three days, my eyes recovered and I could see. The experience of three days of blindness of my life was really scary, with very few friends around. My friends were staying with me these three days in the hospital to help me to go to the bathroom, wash, eat – basic things until my eyes opened a bit and I could see a bit and take care of myself. It was very difficult to not have family, close relatives around you at that time. I had been admitted for ten days in hospital until I recovered from this stupid adverse reaction. How easy someone could take your life away by their mistakes. Discharged from hospital, I had to stay another two weeks at home because of side effects of medication. After two weeks, I was able to go to work.

One bad thing never comes alone. After few months, I again got ill, and no one could figure out what was wrong with me as I was fainting few times per week suddenly. After several tests and investigation, still not diagnosed, I continued being ill. I was talking with family back home about this, and they advised me to come back home to the hospital as my sister spoke with some doctor in a hospital. In May 2003, I flew back home on an emergency for treatment and diagnosis to be found. I took the first available flight (when you are ill, you are not thinking forward for future savings and spending). As I arrived back home, straightaway I was admitted to hospital for investigation and treatment, and after couple of months, I was recovered. When I came, my son did not recognise me at first because already two and half years had passed, and we did not see each other. Also, technology was not so advanced to be able to see each other; we communicated just by public phone. I remember I cried of happiness to see him, and my heart broke as my child did not recognise me. Then I explained to him why I am very slim now as he was remembering me medium build with short dark hair. Two and a half years not to see each other was hard, painful for both of us.

With this unpredicted plan, there was still not enough money to start my life there. I had to go back to Israel as I left on emergency and lost my right to have continuity of work visa. In the meantime, I was researching for another contract to go back to work in Israel.

As I was waiting for answers from different agencies, I decided to go to my ex-husband and my house to get some documents and my son's pictures. Luckily, I was escorted because he was trying to beat me and said he would kill me; if I am not his, I should not be anyone else's. Speaking honestly, I was not interested to find a partner as all my goal was to set up a future for my son. I was not a priority, just keeping myself healthy to be able to work to bring him up. With all obstacles, I was determined to go back and finish my plan.

With lots of research and phone calls to the agency, I managed to find one agency which looked promising. In August, they called me from the Bucharest agency office to pay the commission of $5,000 this time – much more expensive than first time. However, I did not have any other option during this time. The person to whom I paid the commission and who was supposed to send me in few days to Israel, took advantage of me as a single woman. He took me in his flat saying that in couple of days he would get the visa and we would go to Israel. So in the meantime, I had been used and abused. I was cleaning, cooking in his flat, was locked in his flat when he would go out and no chance to escape. There was no option to connect with anyone as he took my phone away from me and there was no phone in the house. He was bringing young girls for sex in a group; I had to assist them and bring things on his request. I was shocked and disgusted of everything I was seeing.

This happened for about two weeks until one day, he had girls indoors for his satisfaction and he forgot the keys on the door. I was always keeping an eye on the door for two weeks; as the flat was on the 8th floor, no way to escape by window. Bringing drink and food forward and backwards I had a quick plan when to disappear. When he was in a busier time with the three girls, I managed to escape and ran away as fast as I could. As I ran away, I did not even know where I was, in which part of Bucharest was I; I just jumped in a taxi and asked to take me to one of my relatives which I had in Bucharest and I knew the address. All my relatives were thinking that I left for Israel already, as I could not get in contact with them.

When my relatives saw me in this distressful state I was, they wanted to go to the police to complain about it. I said that we needed to act in a way that I could recover my money or get a visa to go. I knew that if I had to take any legal action against him, then I was more likely not to go to Israel and never recover my $5,000 from him as I did not have any proof except few messages and no phone yet as he confiscated my phone. I was very distressed about all this experience; however, still I found a way with my relatives to contact him and get in agreement with him that he should send me to Israel as soon as possible or I would come with a TV reporter and disclose everything what he doing behind the closed doors, plus the commissions he was taking and not complying with the law.

He promised that he would try everything to send me to work in Israel as soon he could and said to come to the agency and recover my phone and my luggage with the condition not to disclose anything. I put myself together, controlled myself, I went with my relatives to collect all my belongings. I hated this person for what he did to me, but I kept quiet praying that one day he will get back everything what he was doing to women who sacrifice to get work for a better life. Selfish, cruel person, money maker on poor souls. I still had two weeks of stress to wait in Bucharest, and beginning of September 2003, I got the visa to go to Israel and secured a workplace in Tel Aviv.

Chapter 7

As I arrived in the airport in Israel, one lady from the agency in connection with the agency from Bucharest took me from the airport in her car and said that my place of work was already occupied so I had to go to another place vacant in south of Israel. I did not complain as I understood that it took quite a while for me to finally be here, so I accepted and took whatever was offered. The driving to the destination took about three hours. Despite everything, I was happy I got work and I could start to work after so many troubles and recover my money which I paid in commission. As things are never straightforward, going on the unknown place to take a job as a carer for one old lady is not very easy. I never minded working hard, just wanted to have my soul in peace that I will achieve my goal one day after all these bad experiences.

Bad experience did not finish here unfortunately. Workplace was not really set up for worker with a basic standard, such as having a decent bed to sleep and eat as job required 24 hours from 24 hours. I was sleeping in a sitting room on the two-seated sofa, from which my legs would hang out of the sofa. After couple of days, I started to get in a conversation with the neighbours, and I found out that already about 13 carers left the job after a couple of months. I tried to give this a go. I complied with all requests because I needed the work; I had paid so much money to get there, I had no other option. The lady was very happy with me as I was taking good care of her. I was waiting for some support as well as I was promised to get a decent bed for myself for sleeping. However, I was restricted from many things which I would not disclose now.

There were many missiles from Gaza falling constantly, and thus I would check the glass windows at night to see if we still had them as the lady (my employer) was quite sleepless at night because of this. So no rest at nights, no quiet days, no food provided as per the contract which had to be specified. I was eating bread with spread that I bought myself (to be honest, I could only afford very little at this stage). I was cooking food for my lady employer; however, I was not allowed to eat from this food. One morning, I went for shopping to the market in Sderot, and in the market, I saw missiles in front of me. It was another shocking experience. Lucky no one got injured.

During the first month, I continued hoping for changes. One day, I found out from a family member that I came on tourist visa for one month and there might be a chance that I would not have the right to get a work visa. During this time, I thought that this was the end of my dream to work and recover my $5,000 which I had paid to the agency as a commission. This made me sleepless during the nights thinking of what would happen and how I was going to sort this out. I am a very straightforward person and I also believed that God would help me somehow to sort out this thing and get the right visa for work. Luckily, speaking the language, I got in touch with the Migration Office which provides visa for workers from abroad. I explained the situation how I ended up paying so much money to the agency and they sent me with tourist visa to work. I was very lucky that the people from the Office understood my situation and said that I need to come to the office and put a complaint in writing to sort out this issue.

So one day, I asked for a day off from my employer and went to the Migration office with fear that I could be sent back home. Despite everything, I went trusting in the words people said in the Office and put a formal writing complain about my situation, and I never returned to the previous employer as I technically did not have the correct visa for working. Missiles were falling from Gaza in this area quite often as it was close to the border with Gaza. However, this was not the issue as I got used to this; the most important thing was to get the correct legal documents for work.

After one-month investigation, I received work visa and found work in a prestigious home care in Kfar Shmaryahu where I worked for four years. I was respected and loved for my work by families and colleagues. I worked with one beautiful old lady, very wise. She taught me to speak even lexical Hebrew. She had a beautiful family who always came to visit her and took her for family events. She was a sweetheart. She was loved by everyone who met her as she loved socialising and talking to people. Although work was hard, I never complained. I loved working with elderly people. I was always listening to their stories. Overall, we should not forget that every one of us has a story behind. Thus, I learned to always spend my time carefully listening to the elders. Also, as a new generation, we are learning from them and passing the knowledge to the next generation.

It is incredible keeping the knowledge which passed the Second World War. I kind of knew this already from my parent and grandparents; however, people from this care home had slightly different stories. They told me how they had survived persecution for being Jewish, very difficult times. How many of them lost all their families and arrived in Palestine fighting for a safe and better life? Their life went through a totally different experience in comparison with what we are going through nowadays. I myself had a very troubling experience with my ex-husband, but listening to their story, I felt blessed to be able to come over from afar and to meet and work for them in this care home. All this experience makes me a stronger person and more determined to achieve my goals and find my happiness by working with different people. I was so happy that I had the opportunity to meet and work for these people in Israel for whom I have huge respect.

Spending time with all these wonderful people, I have always wanted to share the experience and knowledge I have learned from them... really never give up your dream, keep trying and you will succeed one day because going through many struggles, I always learned something from each one of them and this made me much stronger and more determined. Wherever you are going and whatever happened, always remain a good person; offer help, work hard and be honest with people and with yourself.

Many times, I felt down thinking of what else could happen before it gets better. Every time I stand up after felt, taking it as an experience and carry on as normal. Because in life, we have to face and deal with all unknowns and uncertainties life throws at us. In 2004, I bought a little flat on my sister's name, then I was hugely relieved that whatever happens with me, my son will have something to remember me for, why I sacrificed so much. I always wanted him to have a roof over his head.

During this time in Israel, I experienced The Second Intifada, also known as Al-Aqsa Intifada, a period of intensified Israeli-Palestinian violence, which Palestinians describe as an uprising against Israel. The violence started in September 2000 after Ariel Sharon made a visit to the Temple Mount, seen by the Palestinians as a highly provocative act. This took place during the period of 28 September 2000 to 8 February 2005.

2006 Lebanon War. The conflict started on 12 July 2006 and continued until a United Nations-brokered Ceasefire went into effect on 14 August 2006, though it formally ended on 8 September 2006, when Israel lifted its naval blockade of Lebanon (34-day life experience of military conflict).

During this period, we were obligated often to handle gas masks that we had to take with us daily. And when the air raid sirens would go off, we knew Hezbollah fired missiles onto Israel, we had to get to the safe rooms called *miklat* or *mamad* (if you had one built in the house). Furthermore, I remember I had my window sealed with cello tape at night when I was going to sleep as well as the door of my room, and the gas mask was always close to me. Many soldiers and civilians lost they life because of this situation.

On 12 July 2006, Hezbollah operatives crossed the Israel-Lebanon border to ambush a military vehicle. Three Israeli soldier were killed and two were captured. When Israelis attempted to find the captives, five more soldiers were killed. From this started a major conflict which ended with 165 soldiers and civilians being killed. After this happened in Israel, I never thought I would be able to come back home one day.

On another side, working for so long, I felt as part of their community and was standing by with them and was ready to help with anything necessary. Although the terror and the attacks, Israel for me always stayed the Holy Land, and I always knew God was with me, thus I never really felt scared. Of course, you need to protect yourself in order to be protected, avoiding places which are under threat and very crowded. On the contrary, you could see also very happy faces, people who respect everybody despite any colour, race, religion or nationality differences where you are working or what you background is.

It amazes me how people find happiness in many little things, as I have always mentioned this to my friends: life is too short for you not to be happy, and you need to live every single day like it could be your last day and learn to be happy with yourself. Daily life is stressful for everybody at any age. Life is also in your own thoughts; your mind needs to understand that life is with ups and downs, never perfect. You could look at the bright side and say: "After a bad day, a good one will come."

I am sharing all of these from my own experience, and I promise you that everything will work if you take initiative for yourself first then deal with the rest. What's important is to not give up and not to always wait for the help from someone else. Everyone is busy with their own life. Sit, analyse what are your priorities, write down on a paper what you need on one side and on the other side what you have (Appreciation list). Failing once, twice, but remember then the third time, I will achieve my goal. Always appreciate what you have not what you do not have. Realise you could be a much more happy person than you think. Always smile because I wake up every morning and I think: *Thank you, God, for another beautiful day.* Take the best of the day and deal with the daily life.

Remember also that everyone has good days and bad days, and we do not necessarily know what other people are going through. Everyone has got daily struggles. This is why I do like comparing myself with anyone because we really do not know what is truly in other people's life. I have been asked many times how I can smile and be so grateful for this life? I always like to remind that I am in a control of my life. I am grateful for what I have got, and I am working hard to get what I need; and I feel that life is better when I am happy and smiling. Also, if I am upset and miserable, I will influence this feeling around me, so I decide to be happy and spread joy to other people to appreciate every single day of my life.

Being happy helps you to go over you daily struggling. With a smile on the face, I would wake up: "What a great day. I woke up, I am going to work, the sun is shining. I have a roof over my head and food on my table. I am so grateful." You feel much better afterwards, everything will go much easier and this inspires other people around as well.

I worked extremely hard to earn money, also took every opportunity to visit the country because it interested me with its incredible history. I also never missed any opportunity for learning anything possible about the country, the people, the tradition and their religion. One thing I can assure everyone is that we are all the same, just we have different conceptions. With an open mind, I found it interesting learning about other people's view on the world and their thinking. My friends are from all nationalities Jewish, Russian, Philippines, Indians, Malaysian, Georgian, Moldavian, and we all were meeting together by the seaside; we were having lunches and dinners together.

We should never judge anyone for what they have, the colour of their skin or where they are coming from. If it is a good person with good personality, we need to love each other and respect each other because this is the only way we could help this world by spreading love around by helping each other and live with happiness on the same planet Earth. Helping someone with a good word, a smile will give you a lot more satisfaction, I promise anyone. Being humble gives peace in your mind, helps you achieve your life purpose. Setting your mind for positive things attracts positive energy. From my own experience, everything I mentioned above happens and is true. I learned to have confidence in myself which helped me to achieve and set my goals. Whatever happened is behind; after a storm, sunshine comes right out.

Many times I was struggling with things that I did not want to disclose to other people, friends, relatives. And not talking about it, I started to write in a notebook which helped me to go through difficult times and make sure I did not get a mental problem. I would advise people who do not like to talk about their problems, write down and that will help you to get out of your mind. Also write your positive thoughts on a paper for what you're grateful and read them every morning when you wake up. I promise you that will help you a lot. I am sharing my own experience with you to help you to get over easier when you struggle and build your mind stronger and healthier.

Chapter 8

Going on a trip to Bethlehem to the Church of the Nativity also known as the birthplace of Jesus, located in Palestinian West Bank made me overly excited as I was traveling with a group using a coach. We arrived at the Palestinian authority checkpoint where we had to present passports for control, and the coach was thoroughly checked as well.

After parking by the beautiful church, we slowly entered. Entrance to the church is low; we had to bend to get in. When entering through this low door, I felt so emotional that I am in the same place where Jesus had been born. For us Christians, Bethlehem, Church of Nativity, Pilgrimage Route are unique places to visit. This beautiful church was built in sixth century AD by the emperor Justinian, in the same place where Jesus was born.

Under the altar is Grotto (the cave) people were queuing to enter, and I joined the queue too. The following area, I discovered during the tour, is the chapel where the big silver star and the stone under where our Lord Jesus Christ had been born. When I touched this Star, I felt my hands shivering out of emotion and excitement. The columns from sixth century presents the design and atmosphere of the byzantine empire era. The mosaic is also original, iconostasis being from byzantine era as well.

As a group, we visited few places that day. Next place was the mountain where Jesus fasted for 40 days and 40 nights, Judaean Desert. Mar Saba monastery, the scenery I found here is based on the complex of house where monks reside and live. The Mar Saba is considered one of the oldest monasteries in the world. Here live approximatively 20 monks who have dedicated their life to prayer and maintaining the monastery. Speaking with one of the monks, he said that their faith is more valued than anything in the world. By listening, his words felt that the personal faith in God is individual and how you believe so you build your faith as well. This monastery has been visited by the Victorian pilgrimage to discover Christianity. Under the Mar Saba monastery lies St John's tomb in a cave.

Next stop, we went to the Mount of Temptation where Jesus was tempted by the devil during his 40-day fast. This monastery is up on the rocks, clinging to the cliffs. We walked approximatively 30 minutes on the steep path to arrive to the Greek Orthodox monastery. It had taken my breath away, the history of the years after Jesus and how priests and monks are keeping these places untouched. Experiencing this stunning view and location has no comparison. The view is amazing as down the mountain are beautiful palms growing in desert, under extreme temperatures.

We continued our journey to River Jordan where Jesus was baptised. Here in Galilee, Jesus preached in his time. Many tourists visit and eat fish here which gives them the sensation that they are experiencing the atmosphere when Peter was fishing in Galilee. The river Jordan's beauty is beyond comprehension; everybody can enter. Therefore, I mustered the courage to enter the river as this was a once in a lifetime occasion. River Jordan holds major significance in Judaism and Christianity beliefs. Furthermore, next to the river is the Sea of Galilee also called Kinneret in Hebrew.

The journey from Bethlehem to River Jordan was an amazing experience. The knowledge accumulated that day; I would like to present it to you in this book so we could enjoy together this beautiful trip.

The years of living apart from my son and family, I experienced so many difficulties and adventures in Israel. I learned to speak Hebrew fluently which led me to participate on TV and radio shows promoting care homes in Israel. I tried to visit all Israel as much as I could due to financial and time constraint. It led me to engage with individuals from various backgrounds and cultures from all over the world who had emigrated during the Second World War, during the time Jewish population were persecuted by Hitler.

Visiting the places known as the last path Jesus has taken to Golgotha, helped me to become stronger physically and mentally, as well as proud and grateful that I was able to see, learn and experience these feelings, experiences and adventures in my life. Life is not easy when you have to work so hard from the beginning, while having to leave everything behind including all material things which I had worked for to achieve. Starting from nothing with a little child seemed like an impossible task; however, I continued with the mindset that I must do it and I will do it. All life has shown me is that nothing is impossible.

My son was growing up in my sister's house. Becoming a teenager, he needed someone closer to be next to him as we all know the teenage years it is difficult for kids as for parents to adjust with changes. My sister advised me that it would be much better if I could be with him this period because she worried that she was losing control over him. He has particularly good instincts and mentality towards learning; however, the period of growing up implies changes on children without parents. They cannot be controlled by other relatives. As an advice, she proposed to come home to discuss my son's future, to speak with him personally to understand each other and plan together.

Chapter 9

I came home on holiday from Israel for two weeks to see my son and my family, to see my parents as they were ageing and not feeling well, also to discuss with my son what he would like to do for his future. He had seen on the TV what was happening in Israel and he showed no interest for this country, as I proposed to take him there with me. After long discussion with him, we agreed to go to UK. I needed to move there, find the job, and bring him over when he would finish secondary school. That was one of the options which he was happy with. For me, it is another start from the beginning, new language, new country but end of the day it's another community with maybe a different mindset than Israel. I was open minded to go ahead and integrate in a community as I did in Israel.

Two weeks had passed, and I was returning to Israel. I went to say goodbye to my parents. My dad had a stroke few years ago; however; he recovered partially. He was managing to move around the house, together with Mom spending their retirement. I never saw my dad crying in my life; however; when I was leaving, that time he cried and said:

"Go my child with God because I do not know if I will see you again!"

"Daddy, do not say that because you passed the worse time; I will see you next time when I will come," I replied.

Its more than 13 years since this happened and I never will forget his words. I did not realise that time why he was saying that to me as I was leaving the country, looks like he was feeling that he will not be with us for long.

12 July 2006 – 14 August 2006

The 2006 Lebanon War, also called the 2006 Israel-Hezbollah War and known in Lebanon as the July War was a 34-day military conflict in Lebanon, Northern Israel and the Golan Heights. With military instability, I was going back to work as I had to plan next step of my life with faith in GOD and going back.

I returned to work in Israel with the worry that I must plan another chapter of my life, more high responsibility as my son would be with me and take responsibility as mother and father, morally, financially with no help from anywhere. I continued to work hard, no days off, working as a babysitter with four kids to save as much as I could for the future move. During this period, I researched and found out that from January 2007 would be free movement to UK for Romanian citizens.

I was saving every penny as I was preparing a plan for moving to the UK. I needed to make sure I had enough money to pay the rent until I find a job, try to learn English language a bit. It's difficult because I am speaking Hebrew perfect; now to start with another language it's not easy as I am in my 40s. With the colleagues at work I was trying to learn a bit, as it is essential to be able to communicate. Considering I can speak four languages fluently, I could not believe I would have such a difficulty to learn English language as I learned in six-month basic speaking of Hebrew.

After New Year, I was researching and planning how much capital would I require in order to have time to learn the language, find the job and be ready to migrate. I knew that I would need to act this year to plan, to settle, to be able to take my son over to UK once he finished secondary school back home. Over the Easter, I went to Jerusalem, visited all places around, went to the churches to thank God for all the help and strength to be able to move on and plan for the next chapter in my life.

It was summer, hot weather reaching 40 degrees Celsius. I was enjoying the last summer with beautiful smell of flowers and the breeze from the sea. Every moment being in this beautiful country amazes me. I have also my friends and told them that I would have to move to UK for my son's future. Everyone was surprised by my all efforts just doing right for him and never counting my own needs. Because I felt it is my responsibility to do everything because I am the mother and father in our family, hoping to do the right decision that will reward me one day. All my Jewish friends were really surprised how much one mother could sacrifice for her child, going from her own country to work abroad, learned the language, integrated in the society in that country. Then move to other country and start from beginning, learning the language, find a job, settle and to be ready in a 1–2 years to bring my son to UK and offer all education possible to be integrated in society with respect and dignity. My brain was saying that if I could speak already four languages then I would be able to learn another new language; whatever it will take, few months or years, definitely I will do it. Power of dream and determination never stop when you are relying on yourself for everything and never you will be disappointed. I started packing and prepared for departure from the care home where I worked.

2007, I lost my favourite lovely old lady Rachel who taught me to correctly speak the language and the one who was the most loved in the care home. She was one of the most beautiful old lady I saw in my life. And ageing, it got her beauty as well; just depends how people see it and comprehend it. I will give advice to anyone that never ever underestimate old people because we all will arrive in that stage when we will need help and to be cared for. Having patience for them (elderly), you must listen them and give them the same credit and respect as the one you would like to receive. The family of this lady was amazing. The love and time they were giving her is to be appreciated and taken as an example from them. I admire their compassion for their mother and grandma caring, respect, keeping her integrated in a family is really valued. The children and grandchildren always took her to special occasions to celebrate together as a family. Working with her gave me so much determination and knowledge for life.

That morning when she woke up, she told me that she was going to join her mother and her husband! I could not believe that she knew she was going to the other world. Now I understand that some people get the feeling when their time to leave our world approaches. I was there for her till the last minute of her life, after resuscitations with AED she left our world. When I closed her eyes forever then I felt emptiness in my soul. Our lives are so precious; we are not happy when we have health, family around, that is the most wealth what we can have. The rest comes and goes through our life. I will never forget this moment of my life, will carry them with me as long I will be alive. Still seeing the lovely family when I am going to Israel.

Chapter 10

Landing in Heathrow airport in the morning of October, I felt the sharp cold in my body as walking out into the unknown, being able only to speak limited amount of the language and looking for direction to the nearest exit where I could find taxis. First thing I noticed was opposite direction of cars circulation compared to other countries where I used to live before. I walked towards the taxi asking to take me to Greenwich where I would be meeting one of my friends. Took me nearly two hours to get there, paid £98 for taxi then walked to the hotel where I would stay until the next day, as I had had prearranged rent for a room in a shared house (setup from Israel) in north London, a place called Harrow on the Hill.

Next day, I travelled to north London to the house where I had rented a room from Israel. There were three couples in three double rooms and myself in a single room with measurements 2.5m x 2m, and only could fit a single bed, a little wardrobe, and little space to walk next to the bed. For three days, I stayed indoors in order to adjust to UK climate and temperatures as the abrupt change of climate made me feel the sharp cold due to high humidity. Therefore, 4th day I went to the shopping centre and bought myself proper jumpers and jackets for cold weather. The cold was getting in my bones because of the high humidity, coming from 35 degrees heat suddenly to 10 degrees, I was feeling the cold.

Following day, I started to go to the agencies to ask for potential vacancies. As soon as I could find work, it would be better for me as I could save the money I came with. Unfortunately, few days in a row, I visited agencies and no luck for work as I did not speak English fluently; I only understood basic amount of the language and was constrained in ability to speak English. This was one key problem. I put announcement in a local newspaper, went to the houses that put advert for jobs, went to interviews; however; the language barrier was working against me. I applied for tens and tens of jobs; however, I was rejected for my level English being inadequate. Therefore, I bought dictionaries and learned everyday bit by bit to get to the stage where I could communicate easily in English to be able to get accepted for a job. In one-month time, day by day I visited all agencies across London to find work. Impossible as I did not speak enough English – rejection after rejection.

One day, I received a call from someone that read in a newspaper that I was looking for a job. I answered happy thinking I would be getting some work. We arranged a meeting in a coffee shop one evening at 7 p.m. As an honest person I was expecting everyone to be honest. I went for the meeting with hope.

"Hello, I am Cristian."

"Hello, I am Dora; nice to meet you."

"I see that you are looking for a job in London?" said Cristian.

"Yes, Cristian, I am looking for a job. You said that you got your business and are looking for workers; could you tell me, please, what kind of business you have?"

"Yes, I employ female escort for hotels around the country."

"Sorry, I think I am the wrong person for that job as I am in my 40s and don't think that is an appropriate job for me!"

"No, Dora. You're perfect with age, looks, everything. I got ladies from everywhere. Come with me to the hotel to see how the work is."

"Thank you very much for your time and consideration, Cristian, but I am not looking for this kind of job."

Immediately, I got up and left the coffee shop because this job was not legal and the proposition was very suspicious considering the large number of human trafficking cases. Sometimes, it is easy to get in this environment but very hard to get out, so better not to get involved. My first hope had gone away very quick; however, I learned that I need to be very firm with people who offer these jobs and not to go with them to see the job because it is easy to become a target being new in a country.

During this time, I found Moldavian agency willing to help me to do paperwork with work permit. I paid £600 but was happy she could help me; also she helped me to register for National Insurance, I went for the interview, and lucky enough, I got it. Step by step, I started to learn how the work was and what paperwork was required for work. In November, I was offered two hours in the morning from 6 a.m. to 8 a.m. with a Lithuanian girl to clean two restaurants, one with three floors and one with two floors, basically one hour for each restaurant. However, we needed the job so we said yes. Living in north and working in south east, that took nearly two hours door to door. So at the end of November, I moved to the hotel in Greenwich to be able to work in O2 Arena. Every day we started at 6 a.m. After two weeks, we had been offered one restaurant more for cleaning and added another two hours which was great for me as I had four hours a day to work. Every single minute that I had, I was learning English from the dictionary.

Due to the busy season of Christmas in O2 Arena, I had been offered a job in a hot dog shop after my cleaning job. Happy that I had found jobs and income, I was waking up at 4:30 a.m. to start work at 6 a.m. and immediately afterwards was going to work in the hot dog shop. By luck, I had a supervisor who spoke Russian, which was beneficial for me as I could communicate fluently in Russian. I was working fast making hundreds and hundreds of hot dogs per day during the events in O2 Arena, and thousands of people were passing through the shop and purchasing. This resulted in me being able to work about 17–18 hours per day in this period. I was happy to work these hours as I knew that I should take every opportunity of work that comes my way. As you never know what to expect in the next day, therefore I was working as much as I could. During this period, I was sleeping four hours per night and I was happy that was good sleep. When returning from work, I never sat down on the bus because I knew I would fall asleep and miss my bus stop. Food wise was very restricted because I was saving for renting the flat for next year when my son would come. I was spending £30 for food per month. Rate per hour was £5 at that time. I was happy I could work, it did not matter which job, just to earn income to support myself and be able to learn the language in the meantime.

My happiness did not last long as my supervisor was off one day and I worked directly under my Turkish manager who sent me to the restaurant to bring some bottles of vodka. However, I didn't understand where in the restaurant and came back empty handed, so he sent me home and said that when I learn how to speak English fluently to come back. For the next few days, I was crying as I lost my day job having just the cleaning one, learning English every minute, with my tears rolling down my face, praying to God to give me strength to go ahead. After couple of days, I was called back to work due to busy time and I was a faster worker in that shop, and they had needed me there.

This experience made me more determined to learn the language, so I would take English course for a year at Greenwich College which would start after new year. In the meantime, I learned from the dictionary myself every time when I got time. Communication is key factor everywhere, so working and having language barrier, it's very hard and difficult. I really value the people who gave me the opportunity to get integrated in the society, had patience with my slow communication verbally, knowing that I understand most of the jobs, am flexible with any jobs needed to be done, and I will do it without any comments. The failures I faced made me stronger, more determined. I learned from my mistakes, kept smiling and tried my best, everyone at work accepting me as I am and assisting me with help making me accepted in a society as a new worker in the UK.

On 11 Dec 2007, I received a phone call from my sister.

"Dora, I have very bad news." I felt in her voice that she was crying. She said:

"Father passed away this morning! Do you think you will be able to come for his funeral? Here it is snowing and snow it is about 50 centimetres, don't think you will have any flights these days as it's going to be snowing for the next few days."

"Please let me check and will call you in a few minutes," I replied.

I checked the flights to go for the funeral. There were no flights for the next two days because of the weather condition. I called my sister back and said:

"There's no chance to get there before the funeral, so just carry on without me."

It's so painful that back home was heavy snow and I was not able to go for his funeral. His words were playing in my mind what he told me when I said goodbye to him as I was returning to Israel. I told them not to wait for me as I would not able to arrive on time as in our religion, those who died must be buried after three days. All family together took the last walk to the cemetery with my father and without me. Time is passing but that memory will live with me as long I live. We must learn to live with our losses; however, we must never forget them. Life is going ahead. I must move on and carry on with my daily life.

Approaching life as it is come, working hard 17–18 hours most of the days, with respect for people I met and helped me with jobs. I will respect them forever that they helped me to learn and integrate myself into the community. I met people from everywhere in the world again. My bosses were from Nepal, USA, UK, Italy, Turkey, South Africa, Kazakhstan, and Lithuania. Working in a large company in the catering industry was a big privilege to be in the UK and work with knowledgeable individuals. Integrated in this environment made me proud to work with them and will always thank them all as I have learned something from everyone. Working in O2 Arena was very cold. As our shop was open to all visitors, on the other side, it was extremely rewarding as you see so many people stop for service, very friendly and respectful towards us. I was serving hundreds to thousands of people in couple of hours daily on the events' days. After working hard, we would be rewarded with free tickets to see few events in the arena which was very nice from our bosses to give us free tickets.

Always looking on the bright side, gave me peace of mind. It did not matter how hard I was working or what I was doing on a daily basis. It was spring; I was getting tired of these long hours and immunity was getting lower. It was nearly Easter 2008, end of April, I became ill, therefore could not work anymore which resulted in all month of May for me to stay home off work, sick.

One of the managers took me from O2 to work in Greenwich in a restaurant since knowing me from O2. Working in Greenwich, I also had the opportunity to start my English course as the hours were much more different; I was starting late and working till late. Now I was having more opportunity to concentrate on my studies doing my English course, and the same time, I registered to take security supervisor course (SIA) as after eight months my English was at basic level. I had belief in myself going for the SIA course to pass the exam and become licenced. As I went to the school where I was supposed to take the course, I was late; instead of arriving at 9 a.m., I arrived at 9:20 a.m. As I approached the teacher, I was feeling shame that I was late when I was supposed to start the course that day. Then my teacher Jon said:

"Mate, you are too late. Go home and come next Monday at 9 a.m. In security, it is important to keep time. At 9 a.m. be in the class, not walk in after 9:00. See you next week here in the same place for the same course!"

"Sorry, I am late. Next Monday I will be on time," I replied and walked out.

With shame that I was late, I said sorry and went back home. I lost that day but with the lesson learned, I went home, taking my books and studying English at home as I could not afford to lose any time off. Following Monday, I learned from my mistake, went to the class nearly an hour early to have time to register and start on time. Timing is important everywhere. I was never late anywhere before this instance. When that happened, then I learned that I need to research before I go to a new place. Taking another qualification would be an opportunity for another job or extra job for future. One small step now could prove to be vital in future. My whole life I have loved to learn everything that I can from people, school, life experience of others which opened my mind towards society needs and be helpful in the society.

After one week of intense classroom, I had the exam. Anxious and full of emotion, I was awaiting the results. After two weeks, I received the email confirming that I had passed the exam and would receive my certificate and instructions how to apply for licence. My first qualification in UK (SIA), after eight months in the country, happy and proud of myself that I have achieved something in the time I spent here. The feeling is amazing when you take one step in the right way but making sure to still comprehend the reality and ambition to learn the language has finally started to show possibilities that can be achieved. Going to the college studying English, I got more confident on my communication with colleagues and customers. I am comfortable to read and understand just pronunciation is tricky which I learned while working in a coffee shop, restaurant and club night as we were changing from restaurant to club on Friday and Saturday nights.

I loved my job, always was smiling and serving customers in the best way I could. Our workplace was busy and challenging almost every day; however, I never complained about anything. Working Fridays, Saturdays and Sundays long hours, finishing Saturday mornings around 2–3 a.m. and starting next day at 9 a.m., my vision for future in UK was strong, and I believed that if was able to stand on my feet, well, then I would be able to bring my son to see himself how the life in UK was.

Chapter 11

My son came to visit me and stay with me on his summer holidays. I paid for an English summer course in Greenwich College for him to learn English. He was excited about it and embraced change very well. After few days seeing how much I was working, he was surprised of the lifestyle I was in. He asked if he could get a little job as well to work a bit. I spoke with one of my friends about it, and he said that he could offer him two hours cleaning job in the morning from 6 a.m. to 8 a.m. As a young boy, I was surprised he agreed to work and after work to go to college from 9 a.m. to 4 p.m. I explained that he needs to be responsible for his work as a 15-year-old boy. I signed for him and gave a try to see his ability.

Surprisingly, for two months, he worked and studied in his summer holiday. He learned to speak English almost fluently during this time. As he had also learned English for seven years with a private teacher back home, he had particularly good grammar knowledge; however, he could not converse in English when he arrived in UK. Giving him better knowledge, I sent him to college to prepare him for next year. I was over the moon that he enjoyed his work and study, and I took him over London to show him the city before he left back to go to finish his last year of study back home. He did not disappoint me; he understood that it is especially important to be honest, work hard and study to be successful in future. When he got paid, he bought himself an expensive laptop in memory of his first job and first time in London.

In August, he went back to my sister for his last year of secondary school. As a mom, I was incredibly happy to see him, spend some time with him after eight years and be proud of him. I kept going to college, working with a smile on my face that I could see my way of settling here.

Christmas time was the hardest time as I was far from family. I was working a lot over Christmas, preparing for big parties in the restaurant, happy to see people enjoying with our service. New Year's Eve I worked from 9 a.m. (31 December) to 7 a.m. (1 January) all day long and all night. I came home, called my family to wish them Happy New Year, then had a shower, little rest, ate something and returned to work at 9 a.m. for few hours as we were open on the first with limited staff available for the day. I never complained about work, was happy I got work and really was enjoying the mixture of all stuff there. After work, we went for a lovely lunch, all colleagues, and treated each other as a family to spend the best time together on the first day of New Year. That time I realised that if we all are happy, then we can have nice quality time anywhere where we are.

February 2009, I finished my English course, took English Cambridge test and passed. Another achievement, slow step but very important for me to be happy for small achievements. I value myself and know to value people around me for having me around them.

Chapter 12

I saved enough money to rent a flat and was getting ready for my son's arrival in June. I moved in a large apartment, still shared but having much more space – not a little room as I lived for nearly two years. During this time, I started to pick up security jobs as well, as I managed to get the licence and needed to get some experience. Applying online for security jobs, had one interview for a nightclub and explained that I had a full-time job during the day, and I was looking for a second job. After the interview, I had been accepted, another happy day to work in different area from catering. I sacrificed every spare time to learn new skills, abilities and experience to work in different places.

In June, I went back for a family wedding and to bring my son to the UK for his education. After long planning and sacrifices made, the time had come. As a single mother, I must be extraordinarily strongminded to not allow my son to go in the wrong direction, as most of the time he would be on his own and there are many temptations in this city. We came back together in June and we applied for his college in Greenwich. He was called to take admittance exams to see if he would be admitted into the last year of secondary school as the system is different in UK from other countries. After he completed the exam, we waited anxiously for the results, and for my happiness and his happiness, he had been accepted as he passed with 99% in Mathematics and 97% in English Language. My dream was coming true slowly and this was a big step was for both of us. As it was summer holiday, I sent him for advanced English course to the college to make sure he was ready for college. Now I needed to make sure I earned enough money to sustain both of us.

He started college in September. I tried to have some free evenings to stay with him to see what he needed to do for his school homework. I made sure he integrates in the school with other kids, spoke with the head teacher to inform me on his status and wellbeing in the school. He seemed to go on well at school, started to make friends which was good. The evenings when I was at home, after dinner, I staying with him to help his preparations for tests and exams which helped me to learn the language with him, as well as I tried to encourage him as much as I could to take school serious, not to be late to classes and not to miss classes because attendance is very important.

In the meantime, he registered himself to a football team as his dream was to play football professionally. After few months, he came from football with his collarbone damaged. We went to hospital, and he needed to have the plaster for a while. After healing his collarbone, he went back to play football.

Working till late in the night, I used to walk from work any time of the night as I used to work until late hours. Walking one day to my friend who used to live on the other side of Greenwich, on the sidewalk I found myself stalked by a man dressed very weird with a bulldog. He said to me:

"You are my woman, and you will be my wife; you need to understand that!"

I felt his breath on my face. I looked at him and smiling replied:

"I don't know you; who are you?"

"I know you very well; I know where you are working, and you are mine!" he replied.

I realised that I was dealing with a man with possible mental issues. He was walking alongside me until I reached my friend on the main road, by the coffee shop. I explained to my friend what happened. She said that I need to be careful with these people as anything could have happened to me and no one would have known. She advised me to go to the police and put it in writing. I thought about it and gave it a go thinking that he would stop stalking me. Surprisingly, it became more frequent. Wherever I was walking, I was followed by him until one day he was with another man similarly dressed and both of them walked with me, and he was saying:

"You are mine, and if you do not come with me and not just mine, then I will kill you!"

This time I got intimidated. Passing the bus stop, bus was on the bus stop so I just jumped on the bus to get rid of them. I followed my friend's advice, went to the police station, and put a complaint in writing about what happened. I described the person, and then was told that he was known by the police with others complaining about him. Nearly one year I had been stalked by this person. Sometimes going for shopping, I would find him next to me, feeling his breath on my side face. I had to be very alert all the time and not show him where I was living. Some evenings my son would come to my workplace to walk home together then he would not follow me. After few weeks I saw that he was not around in Greenwich. Then I found out from colleagues at work that he was looked up for something as he was known for having a gold membership with the UK prison system. It was a big relief not to be worried all the time. As a single woman, sometimes you might experience unpleasant things in life if you do not have the support when you need it from your husband or partner.

I was always working 2–3 jobs to have enough money to pay all expenses for both of us. Some of the neighbours advised me to go to the council to ask for help with my son. I could not do that because I came for his education so I need to pay for everything and help him to get educated. I would feel ashamed to go to the council asking for help as I felt I did not contribute enough yet for the society and economically to ask for help. However, for all the jobs I worked, I made sure I had paid the correct taxes.

I started to lose control over my son for a week. When I was at work on my second job, I called him to check when he got home if everything was OK as I was doing daily. I explained to him why I must work so much as we were in a foreign country and did not have help from anywhere, I needed to provide everything for him and myself. Therefore, he needed to help me by communicating closely to achieve what we planned for his education. As we all know, teenagers think they know better than parents and start to play their games. The same way, my boy started to behave with me. I called my boy maybe 20 times to find out if he was OK because he was new in the country. I was worrying every day when I could not get in contact with him. That day, he decided not to answer me at all, as he went out with his friends from school. I came home from work at 2 a.m.; he was sleeping with no remorse that I was worried all the time during my second job of another six hours shift after normal eight hours shift.

After serious discussion, I said that if he did not comply with my request of having close communication then he would have to leave the country to go back to his dad and I would pay for his maintenance whatever I have to pay but would not accept that behaviour. It was extremely hard; I cried to myself in silence that I try to do everything right and it's so hard, at the same time knowing that teenagers time is difficult and must get used to it. Not showing in front of him how painful this situation was, keeping strong and firm, I gave him two weeks to think what his wish was and what he wanted to do. Next day, he apologised for his behaviour and said that he would comply with my requests and agreed to communicate with me closely. Being tough and harsh as a mother is hard, but it's the way to bring your child on the right pathway. I kept close communications with the teachers to make sure he was attending school on time and his homework was done. He finished his college and started A Levels in the same college; it was good that he did not have to travel far away. So passed two years with ups and downs. He found a job as well in a restaurant so he could earn his pocket money, integrate more in a society and make friends.

Coming one evening from security work around 2 a.m., as I was parking, I was intimidated by two youngsters asking to give them £50. I just said that I am coming from work and I do not have any money on me, and blocked the car doors quickly. They start to swear at me, telling me to get out of the car and many other things. At that time of the night, nobody was on the street and that was under the building where I was living. I did not get out from the car. I was worried for my safety but could not drive as one was staying in front of the car and one next to the window and arguing with me. As the one in the front moved on the side, I accelerated and drove away to the police station and explained what happened. I made the complaint and afterwards went back home. I noticed they were gone. Unfortunately, one of them was my neighbour across the block. After couple of days, coming back from shopping with my son, he passed by and said:

"I am watching you!"

"And police watching you," I replied.

For few years in a row, I was living in fear that one day he would catch me again at night coming from work and do not know what could have happened. After this second bad experience, I decided that I need to learn some more serious self-defence to know how to protect myself. Although I was working in security department, never know what could end up so it would be good to learn self-defence. I found classes of Krav Maga in central London which I attended for the whole week for two hours a day. It was very good training, gave me so much confidence to walk at night. It's very intense self-defence training which improved my strength and awareness of daily life. Knowing how to protect yourself and get out of a difficult situation, it's vital to survive in a city like London, the same for doing job as a security door supervisor at night clubs.

School started again. I was running between two jobs and school. Couple of months since school started, I had already been called to my son's school for him being late or not attending classes. Nearly every week for a whole month, I was called to school to see his head teacher and teacher of economics subject. Being called frequently during the three-month time, on a Wednesday, I decided to sort these issues as I could not afford to be late for work because of his behaviour. That morning at 8:50 a.m., I drove to school with my son to see what was going on and speak with the head teacher first. I spoke with the head teacher and my son in the meeting room and said that they need to call me every morning when he is late because he does not have a reason to be late. When I met the teacher of economics, I was feeling so embarrassed hearing about his behaviour in the economics class and coming to school without homework done. This was unacceptable. In the front of the teacher, I told to my son:

"Sit down and shut up, I am speaking as a parent and tutor. It's shame on you to behave like that with your teacher who is teaching you and preparing you for future. This teacher is helping you to learn important knowledge and skills for future, and I will not allow this behaviour to continue and will monitor closely. I will take appropriate action if you do not follow the instructions from your teachers. Now, please go to the classroom!"

I spoke with the teacher that I would like to receive email with updates on how he is behaving and learning in her classes. Teacher was thankful for being so understanding and taking close action. I explained to her that it is my interest to educate him and really appreciate that she called me in. That was the last time I have been called to school, except parents' evenings. Also, I see improvements in my son's grades and time keeping as well.

Life is never smooth. On a Saturday morning while I was at work, my son went to play football with his team. On a break, I noticed six missed calls from my son and one voicemail. The voicemail was to tell me that he broke his leg at football and he was in a hospital in Kent. *God, what is going on?* I could not leave work until someone came to cover my shift. Going home, I took a few things for him and went to Kent where he was in a hospital with leg broken very bad (bone and ligament completely). Only a single parent can feel how it is to be mother and father, covering everything on my own. Every day, I travelled from Greenwich to Kent to hospital as I could not take him home. Firstly, he could not sit in a normal car as his leg was in plaster fully, and secondly, couldn't get him up by stairs to the flat without help. With help from hospital, they sent him home by ambulance and ambulance crew helped him to get into the flat as there was no lift in the building. After a few days, I started a new job. I couldn't afford to stay home to take care of him; I was paying a friend to come to help him a bit.

One problem does not come on its own, I was walking down the stairs and one of my heels got stuck in my long coat, then I fell down seven stairs. I could have been killed if I fell with my head towards the handrail, I damaged my knee very badly and had bruises all over the body. After siting about 15 minutes full of blood, I got up and limped home to treat myself. I cleaned my knee, put a bandage and stayed at home. My son was with his leg broken; he was telling me to go to hospital because I needed stitches. I did not go because I was in probation still at work and was worried I would lose the job. At work, my colleagues saw that I was limping and started questioning me. I didn't say anything and carried on working until I had to go to the doctor to get some antibiotics because my knee got infected. I carried on working in pain but no one knew what I was going through. That's why I always say, never judge anyone because we don't know what's going on in their life. To be kind and understanding with others is a big help for people who suffer in silence. I was working my second job as a security door supervisor for night clubs and had the privilege to work for many important people for meetings, parties and all different type of events.

Working hard that summer, I took my son on holiday to Spain for seven days; beautiful places, we went around the country, seaside and visited many places. From there, we flew to Paris for three days, another beautiful city with lots of interesting places to visit. I tried to provide the same life as other kids who got two parents, so he did not feel that he was growing up just with me. The time spent together helped us to understand each other better, and I tried to encourage him about life that everything that we want in a life, we can achieve by working hard and having good education. Having close time together, I could approach him more closely. Open discussion with a teenager is very important to know that for good and for bad, we need to trust each other.

In the meantime, I met a man named Gerry at a party and said that maybe I would try to have someone in my life as my son is grown now and understands how life works. My son always said that it would be nice to have someone in my life after so many years on my own. As I was not drinking, smoking or partying, I needed to have something for myself.

After going on few dates with Gerry, I invited him for my birthday party to get to know each other more. It was a nice birthday party, and all my friends liked him and I was happy they met him.

After a few days, he mentioned that he was going to Manchester to pick up the car he bought and asked if I could come with him, and I said yes. I was very excited about the trip. I went because when you want to get to know someone, then you need to spend time together. We went together to pick up the car. On the way back, he asked me if in future I would like to move together with him in the Kent area as the houses are not very expensive there and we could live together. Everything was looking very promising till we went to park his car in his lady friend's house. I met his friend who was not very happy about my appearance, but I thought maybe it was a wrong impression as I met her the first time. We went to his flat, had dinner and were chatting, but his phone was constantly vibrating as his lady friend was texting him. As he told me she was only his friend, I didn't take any offence. We woke up in the morning, and our plan for Sunday was to go to the seaside. I saw straightaway strange behaviour from my boyfriend. After having coffee, he asked me:

"When I am going back home?"

"As we discussed before, I will drive back to London on Sunday evening," I replied.

We prepared his van and he had a jet ski, so we were preparing to go to the seaside. He told me that he was just going to one neighbour to pick up something for the van and would be back. I went outside by the house where he lived waiting for him to return. Half an hour passed, and he didn't return. Then after an hour, I tried to call him, and the phone was switched off. I went around to his neighbourhood; no sign of his van anywhere. I understood that something was not right. For my luck, I had my things with me and car keys as well in my handbag so I drove to London. I couldn't understand what was wrong and where he went. I tried to contact him to ask what was wrong, why he left me outside and ran away; as grown adults, we could have a conversation.

After a few calls and messages, I asked him to meet to talk about what happened. To my surprise, he went to the police and lodged a harassment complaint against me for wanting to talk with him. This shocked me and I could not believe it, not because he didn't tell me what was wrong but going to the police and lodging a complain about relationship communication, UNACCEPTABLE! I went to his local police station and requested them to call him and confirm the basis he put the complaint against me. I wanted to put on record all the true facts about what happened. I knew I didn't do anything wrong and would not take the blame for nothing. Police recorded all the information regarding this. I said that I would not contact him again but also would not allow false accusations on my record.

GOODNESS ME! This was the beginning of other things to follow. When we were together, we booked training for close protection together. When I contacted the instructor from training, I received an email by mistake with all attached information what he sent to the training company about me. I was shocked! He stated that, "I have been picked up by the police and sent back to my country, so will not be able to take the course." I contacted the training company and explained the situation regarding the statement provided by this man on what happened, and I confirmed that I will attend the course as I currently have a British passport and never had any issues with the police except this instance with the false accusations and lies made up by Mr Gerry. Considering all that had happened I was determined to attend the course for the whole 16 days, irrespective if Mr Gerry attends or not. Nothing would stop me if I don't have anything to hide.

Arriving to the course, we had been accommodated in the same hotel. Knowing that I did not do anything wrong, I would continue with my life and disregard Mr Gerry's existence in the hotel and course. He tried to talk to me like nothing happened and offer me things. I refused any offer from him. I finished the training, and the last day everyone was saying goodbye from each other as we were eight students, seven men and myself a woman. I did not regret going for that course as I learned a lot and had courage to face him the whole time. I never ever saw this person in my life again and don't want to meet him again as trust and honesty is very important in life.

I grew up in a very straightforward family where we were taught not to lie and be dishonest; we had been taught that with lies, you never will succeed and will feel ashamed. However harsh the truth is, I will happily face it but will not tolerate lies and dishonesty. After this experience, I moved on with my life, having family and good friends next to me. After receiving my Close Protection Licence, I worked for foreign MPs, VIPs, princesses of Dubai, Mr Bean filming; great experience and proud of the jobs I did. I always learned something from every job and tried to bring the best service for the clients I worked for. In the meantime, my son finished A levels and will go to university in Cambridge. I am happy that my dream slowly came true.

Chapter 13

Beginning of 2013, I went to Israel with my friend Alyn, for ten days, and we had nice good trip there. First we stayed in Tel Aviv for few days and then we went to Jerusalem to visit the old town of Jerusalem.

As we were visiting around, we got to the Dome of the Rock located on the Temple Mount, an Islamic shrine in the Old City of Jerusalem. To our disappointment, we were not allowed to visit because we were not Muslims, even though we were dressed appropriately to visit. My friend being a history teacher was very disappointed that she could not visit this place. I was disappointed as well because Dome of the Rock got one of the oldest extant works of architecture. Architecture and mosaics were patterned after nearby Byzantine churches and palaces. Outside changes had been made with gold-plated roof in 1959–61 and again in 1993.The octagonal plan of structure is similar to Byzantine Church of the Seat of Mary (also known as Kathisma in Greek). Dome of the Rock had been built between AD 685 and 691 by the caliph Abd al-Malik ibn Marwan on the road between Jerusalem and Bethlehem.

We then went to Garden of Gethsemane, the place where Jesus came with his disciples and went to pray. The olive plantations were kept in the same format as the one used 3,000 years ago. It's the same garden where Jesus was captured before crucifixion. Just new ramification coming from under old, dried covers. We enjoyed every single moment there, meeting people from around the world visiting the touristic attraction.

After we visited everything in Jerusalem, we returned to Tel Aviv and then we travelled next day to another beautiful place which is the Dead Sea. We took a minibus to Jerusalem and then changed for a coach to the Dead Sea. This was a relatively long journey but worth every penny. We arrived there, and then I left my friend in a coffee shop and went to find a hotel where we could stay overnight as we hadn't booked in advance because it was not season time. However, we realised that the area is busy the whole year, so it would have been better to pre-book ahead.

I found the hotel in the end, hotel Isrotel Ganim, where we stayed for five days – beautiful hotel with a pool, jacuzzi, saltwater pool, massage and mud and beauty therapy. Dead sea is a salt sea, bordered by Jordan to the east and Israel the West Bank to the west. Dead Sea dates since over 5,000 years ago. Brilliant experience as we went to the sea. Being march, we were expecting the water to be cold; however, the water was warm enough to go in and stay in the sunshine. After two days, we went to visit Ein Gedi, the spring waterfall park. Walking to the park, it was a beautiful sunshine day as we walked with other people to the park, visiting all points of spring waterfall then instead to come back to the park down where was spring water, we followed the other tourists to the claiming rock attractions. Without realising we began claiming rocks and we went quite up. We realised how hard and dangerous, rocks were abrupt, slippery, no holding rail or anything and there was no way back. We must keep going to the top of rocks and find another way to go back down. My friend looked down as we have been about 5 miles up, she asked:

"Dora, if I fall here, will you take me back to England?"

I was worried enough, as she had medical problems, to get her safely, and after her question, I became more worried. I just told her:

"Don't look back, as I am behind you. Just look forward until we will get somewhere safer."

After about three hours climbing, we were exhausted. We stopped on the way. Younger individuals were climbing quicker, but for us, it was more difficult. We were so happy we arrived at the top with a beautiful view in our sights. We sat and had a rest, admired the beautiful view which made it worthy to get to the top. People was looking so little from that high altitude, one side Dead Sea with its royal blue colour with white sandy beach, the other side was the national park and mountains of Jordan.

On the way down, we went on the other side, which was a nice and comfortable way to go down plus we saw the Chalcolithic Temple of Ein Gedi and a Ghassulian public building dating from approximatively 3500 BCE. Another beautiful place from Byzantine period which was the synagogue mosaic remains from Ein Gedi's including a Judeo-Aramaic inscription. Ein Gedi literally translates in English as 'spring of the kid' which is an oasis and nature reserve in Israel, located west of the Dead Sea, near Masada and the Qumran Caves. The village also known as kibbutz was founded in 1953. It was named after the Biblical Ein

Gedi, located on Tel Goren beside the kibbutz which was an isolated village from the city. After the 1967 Six-Day War, Israel captured West Bank from Jordan then made a paved road from Jerusalem via Jericho and along the shore of the Dead Sea opening the door to tourism.

On the way back, we decided to cross a beautiful palm plantation. As we were taking pictures, I spotted something moving in the ground and stopped to look as my friend was walking across the plantation. It looked very strange but I just carried on and we headed to the hotel. We explored every single minute of the Dead Sea as we know it is a very rare place in the world. The view was amazing because as I turned, in different positions, there are different views, from mountain, plantation, hotels and sea. The sand is so fine that walking on the beach is a pleasure, using blue mud for therapy and float on the top of the sea is all what me and my friend experienced in this beautiful place.

After a few days, we returned to Tel Aviv to fly back to UK from there. As our last evening in Israel, my friends invited me for dinner with all her family. I was saying where we went, what we visit in the Dead Sea, then I mentioned that I saw it something weird in the plantation. They asked me:

"Did the plantation have a sign of 'No Entry'?"

"Yes, we just took a short cut to the hotel," I replied.

At that point I saw their faces dropped and my friend's husband shouted at me:

"Did you have enough of your life? Do you know you two could disappear forever and nobody would know what happened with you! There were some ground holes detected; that's why they closed that palm plantation."

We remained completely astonished by the news and also by how lucky we were not to fall there. I did apologise to my friends for ignoring signs and promised that I would take their advice for future reference. Next day, we returned to UK.

Chapter 14

I was preparing my son for university and looking for accommodation. In September 2013, he started his university. As a mother, still my job was not finished yet. I was still working two jobs, and every second weekend a month, I was driving to Cambridge to my son's accommodation to bring him cooked food, fruits, everything that he needed to know he eats healthy because he was working as well during the university time. My journey from London to Cambridge for three years was an exciting and happy journey. I never complained; just carried on till I saw my son graduated. I wish I had a partner or my son's father to help me over these years; however, I achieved my goal to bring him up, give him good education and integrate him in society with good manners, knowing the truth, it is very important in daily life.

In 2014, I was still working two jobs; however, I managed to go on holiday in a hot country as I suffer with asthma. Normally, for this condition, it is very helpful to stay at least 7–10 days by the seaside. I used to go in the mornings and evenings and walk for 40–50 min every day which I can confirm really helped and kept my asthma under control for years. I was really lucky during this year as I managed not only to visit Israel but Portugal too. With happiness in my soul that it was my son's second year of university, I never missed the opportunity in Israel to go to the church in Jerusalem and give thanks to God for His help toward this year. I also find that place where Jesus is buried very peaceful, calming, giving me power and determination for everything that I am doing. Personal belief is very important in someone's daily life because we are all different by colour, religion, nationality, but one thing we have in common is that we come without anything on this world and leave without anything except the memories, good deeds behind us.

This year was a painful year for me which left me with something missing in my soul. I used to talk to my mum on Skype frequently. In October, as it is a National Cathedral bank holiday, I called my mum. She was at my sister's house, as Christmas was approaching. I asked what she would like me to send her for Christmas. She answered that she has got everything; she just wanted to be healthy and she was not sure she would still be with us by Christmas. I got upset with her answer; however, we changed the subject and continued the conversation. Not long after this conversation, I received a phone call from my sister that my mother was in a hospital; she had a stroke overnight, 11 November 2014.

I took a holiday from work and went to see my mother, I stayed in the hospital with her for seven days. After that, the doctor said that she could go home and recover at home, which personally I think was not a very good idea as we paid so much money to the doctors for having good treatment and care. Saturday evening, we arranged in mother's house to call the priest to read from the Holy book and pray together for her health. When priest opened the Holy book, standing behind, I saw that the page where it was opened, majority of the letters were in black colour but just some letters were in red; I felt that she would not be long with us. Heartbroken about it, I just continued and encouraged her to believe that she will recover. As a family, we knew that she will not be for very long with us. I came back to the UK because I had work, with sadness that soon I would lose her.

On 19 December, I received a phone call from my sister that she passed away and the funeral would take place on 21 December 2014. That was the hardest time when I lost my mum. Does not matter my age or her age, I can confirm it is the same pain because this is my mother who gave me birth, life, brought me up, taught me what is good and what is bad and made me who I am now. I flew with the first flight available back home for her funeral. She was looking so real like sleeping. I sat all night long next to her coffin to enjoy her beauty for last minutes in this world. I will never forget those last minutes. Feeling orphaned without her, I returned to the UK on 23 December 2014, switched off my phone and stayed indoor all Christmas grieving in silence. I know she is in a better place now, have to accept the loss and live life. As we know, we are in transit in this world so we have to take it as it is and go on with daily life. On 2 January 2015, I returned to work.

Chapter 15

In January, I applied and sent all my paperwork for becoming a British citizen. I passed all tests required for application with no problem. I always thought for eight years I have paid more than double in taxes to HMRC; I was really hoping to be approved. My happy news came end of January. I received a letter that my application was approved and I received an invitation to the ceremony beginning of February. This day was the best day of my life in London. I was very honoured that I was becoming a British citizen. I went to the ceremony and received my Certificate, and beginning of March I received my British Passport. This was the biggest achievement in seven years which filled me with honour that I am part of the country, and thanks to my hard work, I got rewarded with integration in the community. All this journey I did on my own, with my family's support morally which really helped me, was really rewarding.

I continued working 2–3 jobs, making time every 2nd weekend to go to Cambridge to see my son, taking him a lot of fresh cooked food, fresh fruits, soft drinks, bottles of water and more what he needed. As a mum, I never complained I was too tired or did not have time or did not feel well. I always was going there, making sure he was living in a good condition, helping clean the kitchen in their student shared accommodations to have good standard of life. Not many parents were doing what I was doing, but for his health, I was taking extra steps.

Beginning of June, I went to holiday in Spain in Alicante with friends for few days. It was an amazing experience. We visited museums, palace, beautiful beach places. One day, I heard music from the beach and said to my friends we should go to visit. It was a dance fiesta, which was taking place every year and was very interesting as it was showing Spanish tradition. It was an amazing experience. As I spoke several languages, I was able to translate to my friends what they were celebrating. I was always fascinated how people are keeping their tradition from generation to generation. As good time always goes, it finished quickly, and I returned back to daily life. I was back at work, refreshed and ready for the long hours. I planned that this would be the last year that I would be working in 2–3 jobs as my son would finish university next year then I would be able to live with one job.

At work, I was nominated for an award (Women in Security) which was a true representation for my hard work and commitment at work. I was invited to an interview with one of the directors. After being shortlisted I was formally invited for a dinner in a lovely hotel in Central London where they held the reception for the annual awards. All of my bosses came with me for the dinner and supported me for the award. Great evening! I really would like to thank everyone who recognised me and supported me during this lovely achievement. My interview was published in the company website as well. All these achievements helped me in developing myself more and more.

During the same year, I registered myself for another course, Supervisor Leadership Academy. Also, my son finished his university and had his graduation ceremony. It was the happiest day; my hard work was paying off and my goals were finally getting achieved. I was so happy to see him getting his Diploma in the hand by his teacher and being dressed in that lovely gown. What could give more happiness to a single mum than seeing her son finishing education which she had always dreamed of becoming reality. I would again personally thank everyone who helped me during this journey (my sister with her husband, my friends) and thank God for giving me the power and the strength to overcome all obstacles. I will advise every single parent to never to give up on their dream and goals because everything can be achieved. You need to have determination for anything you want.

At the end of the year, I had a phone call that my best friend from Israel had fallen and was not feeling well. I was over the phone with her for few days, then after New Year, I booked a ticket to see her. I flew immediately after New Year to see her as she had been admitted to hospital. I arrived on Tuesday, went directly to the hospital and finally found her. She was over the moon to see me, and we had a long chat that evening. One thing I was not happy about was that she had her phone taken away by her next of kin and she could not contact anyone from her friends or family though she was able to talk and had a clear mind. On the next day when I came to see her, she was in coma, and during the night, she passed away. I was heartbroken and upset with myself that I had not gone earlier to have spent more time together. Her death hurt me a lot because it was too soon and unknown. The question I had was never answered, why she had her phone taken away from her and any of her friends or family did not know she was in a hospital. However, I will probably never receive this answer. I learned from this mistake to keep close with your family and friends and go to see them more often so it's not too late. I was not able to go for her funeral as I had to return to UK to work.

My son started his new job in Cambridge. Now I was looking for my new start of life, maybe to meet a nice person to age together. As I was living alone, I started to go out with my friends. Middle of June, I went to a Singles Dinner party with my friend and met Josh. When we met, he said he got three kids. I always liked a big family as I myself was from a big family, so that was actually quite an interesting fact for me. We met again and we tried to know each other. We went on different dinners and lunches together to find out if we got things in common and if we could enjoy each other's company. As I was in my 50s, I was expecting to meet someone of a similar age to have similar interests of life, to be with someone then we could potentially age together. I was missing family life. Because of being so many years on my own, I was looking forward to meeting my other half.

We had an evening out and had a really good time. He said he was very in love with me, was very happy that we had met and would like to spend rest of his life with me. That was a very early stage to hear such strong words from someone who you have met the 3rd time. However, I trusted him blindly. He said that he was a victim of his previous partner, that she took their daughter away from him; his parents are old and cannot see their grandchild. In this, I found actually he had four kids not three. However, this did not change anything; I was just wondering why this was not mentioned at the beginning. Blindly in love, I believed everything, supported him on his case in court to win his child to be able to see her. I started to visit him as his house was out of London. When I was off, I was spending time with him. He was a man with a very serious job, and I expected that everything that he was telling me was true; I believed everything.

Meeting with his family, I started feeling that I could get integrated in a family. I visited his parents who were in their 90s and were the sweetest old couple I have ever met. I loved them, went to bring some cooked food couple of times on the way to my darling Josh (at that time!). I respect old people; we all are going to age at some point and we know they really appreciate a visit from someone to have a bit of chat and help them. As we kept seeing each other, I really enjoyed his company. After a few months, he said that would be better if I move in with him in his house and we would be together. I asked what would be the conditions if I moved in? He said that he would need to give his ex-partner money for her part of the house then I could buy her part for myself then we could live together – which was reasonable. And the first few months, I would not need to contribute anything towards the house mortgage until I find a proper job as I would move out of London; since this would be hard and expensive to commute, I would look around the area to find something closer. I was supposed to travel to Australia in December so he was saying that it would be better if I move in before I go, why pay rent if I am away and so on. Being blinded in love and nobody to advise me, he persuaded me to move before Christmas, before my holiday.

Chapter 16

So I moved in with goodwill that I found my partner for life after being single so long, waiting for my son to complete his education. We were going with both cars to pick up the last things from my flat. I was going to give the keys to my landlord. On the same day, I spotted something wrong which got me thinking whether I took the right decision but was too late as I had 99% moved in.

During that day, he was expecting a delivery, a present for someone. As we were driving out of his town, we stopped at the petrol station to put petrol in the cars. He said that he needed to go back because the delivery driver left his parcel out and this was an expensive present; he was just going to put it indoors and would be back, just to wait for him there. As I had been told, I drove to the side in the petrol station and was waiting for his return. After 20 minutes, he returned, and we drove to London to collect my last furniture from my flat. It was a busy day, coming together with all my stuff. I was thinking that I would do my best to make this work and be together forever. After dinner, he showed me the present, a present for a family birthday. We went the following weekend for that birthday and gave him that present and we had nice evening. His kids did not really like me, but I tried my best to respect them as my kids because I always said that kids do not need to suffer because of parents' divorce or separation. I loved all family because I believe if I love their dad then I need to love them as well, and with my hand on my heart, I can say I did love all his family and his ex-wife who was a very good-hearted women.

I finally found new job. It was closer and a very prestigious job; just the pay rate was lower than my previous job. However, for love I had gone for this job with my boyfriend's knowledge and to be closer to home. In few days, I went for my long-planned holiday to Australia. I tried to get in touch every morning and evening with my boyfriend to tell him where we were going, what we were doing as I was thinking this was normal. Over Christmas, we had a video chat with all his family from his house and his little child was waiting for me to return. I loved his little child as my child. I brought up my son on my own, and I always said that kids do not have any guilt of what happens between parents and was looking after her like after my own kid. We were video chatting constantly until my return from my holiday.

I got back to Heathrow Airport and waited for two hours until he arrived to pick me up. However, things happen so many times so I let this pass and avoided unnecessary conversation. We had some discussion in the meanwhile as I was thinking we were beginning to know better each other as we did not live together for long, and after all, I changed jobs in to be closer to his house, to spend more time together. After a few days, the delivery van arrived and the delivery man was asking about a parcel that was delivered on that specific day because Josh said he did not receive this and if I know anything. I remained mute and shocked as I knew exactly that this parcel was given as a present already.

When Josh came home, and I told him that the delivery company came asking about the parcel which had been delivered, and they investigated because you said that you did not receive it. He turned 360 degrees and said that I should not talk to anybody because people are not genuine nowadays. This was a horrible day knowing that I had to live with someone who was not straightforward. I was desperately trying to save my relationship, trying to forget what was bothering me, and yet I could not do anything about it. I risked everything, my movement from London, my job from Central London, my freedom so I was still trying to get over this thing.

In the meanwhile, property agents were coming to evaluate the house. I kept asking how it was going as I knew he kept going to the tribunal for his case with his ex-partner whom he needed to pay for the other half. I kept asking but did not get any answer – still ongoing. I was never told the reality. All my stuff had been put in another room and locked. This was shocking to me when I tried to go in as I needed something from my boxes. When I asked why my belongings were locked, I had been answered that his documents were there that's why he was locking. Straightaway, I felt this was not right. The trust was not there. I trusted him to move in his house and he was locking this room with my stuff in and keeping the keys in his pocket all the time. That day he made me feel angry, upset that I was treated like a stranger in his house.

Then this opened my eyes further to see what was happening and find out what I got into. When we were home together, he was always on a computer in the other room, closing the door behind so that I did not see what he was doing on the computer. I know that if I share my life with someone, I would never hide anything. With Josh, this was not the case. As I opened the door, the screen would go down, he would close what he was doing, and all papers around him, he would turn on a blank page or hide. This got me more concerned about what was happening. Past few months, property agents stopped coming. I asked what was happening; the answer was still not sure what will happen. I let go everything as I wanted to avoid any unnecessary discussion because if he got angry, he would not talk to me and would verbally abuse me. I tried to avoid that.

He finally got first custody for his little child and now he had to attend parent course as compulsory for his child custody. After this course, he started being more on his phone than normal. As a woman, I felt that he might have another woman because my phone was always displayed and I once when I offered to answer, I was not allowed to touch his phone. I felt that there was something going on in his life as his behaviour was changing, and he was more on the phone than normal.

On Easter day, he said that one of his friends from USA came to see his parents and said that he would like to see him as they had not been in touch for a while. Obviously, who is leaving his family on Easter day to meet a friend? Was too obvious of a lie. However, I tried to explain that this is Easter day and we should spend together but it was too late, because he wanted to go. He asked me to iron his shirt and trousers because he was going to see his friend in London (?). Sunday 12 o'clock he had gone to London (?) to meet his new girlfriend. I knew it; I felt that on that day was the end of our relationship. Immediately, after he started to see his new girlfriend, he asked me to pay rent per month. However, I was paying all the bills, all shopping for the house; this was never considered. I loved him blindly. I was trying to save our relationship, but I knew he had gone for another woman. I cried during that day; could not sleep either. I walked his dog because animals also have no guilt in human relationships. I loved that lovely dog.

I remember, during one sunny day, I wanted to get one of my summer pairs of shoes which was locked in this room and I got upset about that situation. Then God guided me to this discovery as I was with the dog in the kitchen on my own during Easter day, crying that I compromised so much and my boyfriend had gone to meet his new girlfriend. I suddenly saw a pair of keys on a kitchen appliance. I took them and opened this mysterious door, and for my luck, when I unlocked that door and took my shoes from the box, then I saw all the letters from the tribunal but not from his ex-partner or ex-wife but from another ex-girlfriend whom he had taken to tribunal for some money claim. For my surprise, I discovered all his life history there. What he had told me about himself and what was the reality was quite different. That day I found out everything that he hid from me for nearly a year being together. In short, he was in a tribunal with his ex-partner and his ex-ex-girlfriend. His ex-girlfriend as a single mum accepted to repay him money claimed by Josh, and due to circumstances, the claim had to be paid by instalments of £4 a month for 17 years (this was her budget). Further, there were letters from his ex-partner how he was living with her and with his ex-wife for three years. That day I found myself in the middle of nowhere because I would have been the next one taken to tribunal by him for God knows why.

In the meanwhile, he lost his job after 30 years of service. Consequences started to come, and he was suffering. I still tried to accommodate him, counsel him during this hard period because as a human being I understand how hard it is when you are made so suddenly redundant. I got a good heart; I always help everyone who needed help and I am not regretting it. However, I was not surprised as when you are doing bad things to other people, it always is coming back to you. My heart was broken and my tears during this period never dried. I went to the church Sunday morning and cried in silence, so people do not notice; however, some people saw me and came to me to console me, asking me what happened and why I was crying. I explained that I got in a mess with a man whom I blindly loved and cannot find way out living in his house.

As I came from church, he asked me to help him with something for his car as he was fixing it. I helped and at around 12 o'clock he went again to his new girlfriend. No remorse that I compromised so much to be with him. I left so much behind to be with him, NOTHING! He still used my phone to get in contact with his colleagues as he was not allowed to contact anyone from work when he was redundant. He took me to stay with his parents, clean their house with no remorse he was just using me. On top of everything, he planned a holiday for half-term holiday with new girlfriend and her child during the time when I was still in his house, taking care of his little child and himself. I let it go to avoid conflict as having nobody of my family to help me except my son I had to suffer and try to work things. He still wanted me to go with him and his little beautiful child on a day out. I went with them to many events, just kept happy. I was still cooking, cleaning, shopping just with my money because he was redundant, just for the sake of peace in the house. I loved the little child and she loved me as well. I still keep her pictures and hope one day to see her again. She touched my heart and I still love her, and I miss her.

I started to look for another job and accommodation as I knew that it would come the day I would need to get out. In the meantime, my son was moving all furniture as he got a new flat, empty, and my furniture was staying in the garage as I was not allowed to change anything in Josh's house. So I gave him all furniture for his flat and all appliances for the kitchen.

We started living in separate rooms as he was happy now with his new girlfriend but was not saying anything because he was also happy to have a slave at home to use. One day, I was coming from work and had a car accident, unfortunately. It was shocking for me as it was my first major road accident. The car was completely destroyed. I called him and told him what had happened. He said that he was in his parents' house and not feeling well. His advice was to sort out with the insurance. The shock from the road accident was making me shiver constantly, thus the police was called on the place as I was not able to control myself. People around me were extremely helpful at that moment. One of the work colleagues came to check on me as they heard from someone who passed by that I had an accident. After a few minutes, my manager came and stayed with me, helped me to sort out the car as it was required to be removed from the road. I just took my bag and my manager brought me home in his car.

I got into his house and had to walk his dog because the poor pet did not know what was happening. This dog was my refuge and consolation as I was going for a walk and run with him. Dogs are truly the best friend. He always was next to me although he was not mine; he felt the love. For three days, I was in the house by myself. My lovely boyfriend was away because it was easier to go to his girlfriend from where he was staying. I stayed indoors as I was not able to go to work as I did not have my car, and I was ashamed to disclose to my workplace what was happening. I wanted to rent a car for this period, but my boyfriend came back and straightaway said no because he got his daughter's old car which needed to be used as it had not been used for a long time. Being under his roof, I still had to comply with his orders. I complied with his order, went with him to his parents' house where the car was, and in the meantime, he said to go to clean his parents' house because he had to blow the wheel.

I agreed to his request just avoiding any arguments, still like a blind person, hoping he would drop his girlfriend and be with me. This very often happens when you are in love and another person just uses and abuses you. He was verbally very abusive, so I had been through this already trying to avoid any arguments. So I had to use his relative's car in this time as I would manage to have my car back. To be fair, he helped me to find a garage which repaired my car through insurance, helped me to take it from the garage as well. At this time, I was thinking maybe he would come back to me and we still could save our relationship. There were days when he was genuinely nice. I would still cook and he would sit and we would eat together – very strange relationship. I was still hoping.

However, as usually one thing was not coming alone, I drove to the new interview with this car and, of course, the car being so old and long-time unused, during the drive back home on A505, the car broke down; acceleration pedal burned off. So when I called him to inform what happened, I was told off that it was my mistake. Whatever, I called AAA to rescue me. I was towed and brought home. Again, no car; called the garage and begged them to finish because I was again indoors with no car. After a day, they called that the car was ready for collection. Big relief for me that I would have my car back and knew it was time to sort out my life again.

Monday morning, I changed both beds and as I was putting for washing, I found his shirt full of make up as Sunday afternoon till 3 a.m. he was at his girlfriend's house. When I showed him and said nicely that it is not nice for a dad of four again with a new girlfriend with a kid, and that he was making the children ashamed of him because he was constantly with someone else. He started to shout and scream at me. Then I started to pack and I knew I had to look ASAP to move out. Next day, I went to look for flats around the place where I lived but knowing that it was not good idea to be around. The same day, I was informed that I got the new job, so immediately I changed and went to look for flats in a different place close to the future job. As we had been under tension, I had to make sure that I got home before evening not to be locked out. Still insulted by messages, had to get out as soon as possible.

Friday afternoon, he told me to be home because someone from the council was coming for his complaint made about some issue and I needed to be present for the meeting as I was his witness for that complaint he made. As I was miles away,

I was not sure I would be able to make it but was told that I had to be there by 3 p.m. with no excuses. When I came home, he started to insult me. As the person left, he started shouting and screaming to get out from his house Friday evening! I packed everything and put in the car. Stressed a lot from the situation and insults during the week, I decided that I was scared to stay anymore there. When he saw me with the luggage down the stairs, he requested money which I owed him for the car. As I got out to the car, he locked me outside knowing I did not have the keys. Being so stressed and feeling alone in the world, I called the police because I wanted ASAP to get out from his house as he was insulting me constantly. Police arrived and asked me what happened? I explained that I was taking my stuff and leaving the house because he kicked me out from the house, screaming and shouting at me, and I was scared to stay in his house. I was not feeling safe. Police officers helped me to take my stuff out of the house. I drove off, leaving the police officers with him in the house.

Chapter 17

Crying all the way to my son's place how unlucky I was to be moving the second time in six months. It was shocking for me how I trusted him, and he destroyed me. Heartless person!!! However, I believe that how you treat people, the same you will be treated; one day will come when he will have the same experience which he gave me. God is never sleeping. As I got to my son, I dried my tears, asked him to help me to take all the stuff in and told him that I would be for a while in his place.

Following day, I put myself together, said to myself, *That was a bad experience; I have to move on. Life is too short, need to make the most of it.* Had a coffee and went to the previous workplace to give my uniform back and say goodbye to my colleagues. Everyone was genuinely nice and gave me comfort and said that they would miss me at work and not to be upset because I deserve a man who loves me and takes care of me. As I said that I had not come to work when I had the accident because my boyfriend did not come to see me for three days, my manager remained shocked and said that I really deserve a better man; as I worked with them, they know how I respect everyone and help everyone. That is life. I was sad I had to leave the job but it was better to go away and not to be around.

Back to my son's place, I started to look for accommodation for rent temporarily in a new place and start my life in a quiet place with no stress from someone who you love is taking you for granted.

As I was viewing flats; after five days viewing few flats per day, I managed to find a nice one-bedroom flat in a nice area, and it would be available a week before I would start the new job. Perfect! I never gave up as I had still not done my last dream… then enjoy life. Everything started to take shape again. I put down the deposit for the one-bedroom flat to rent and I was waiting to get the key. In the meantime, I prepared things what I would take over from my son's flat and what I would still leave because he has a big flat with a lot of space.

Single again, but happy; not under stress, humiliated, insulted. I was only missing my friends from London but will make new friends from around here. Does not matter where we are, we're all human beings and need to be nice and friendly to each other. I was looking forward to starting this new job and regaining my happiness. I loved working with people; all my life I worked in the front line. All my life I have been at work. I am proud I could manage to sustain myself always, never been dependent to anyone and never will be. I got my self-esteem to do everything and anything everywhere where required and stand up for my rights.

I got the keys, moved in on my own; my son would only come over the weekend to help me a bit. Now I was just settling down and exploring the area. Workplace was very close, few minutes to drive. Thanks to God how He worked out everything for me. I started work the next day, really looking forward, loved the new place and work as it was with people all the time. I met my lovely colleagues and was looking forward to having nice team and enjoying work together.

Now I needed to find nice flat to buy. I had few viewings but not what I would like. I needed to go around to find more about it. Couple of months later, I found my lovely flat to buy... happy days... Processed my paperwork, put an offer and now waiting for papers to go through. As I said earlier, always after bad day comes, something good awaits. This is why I never look on the bad side of what is happening because I do not want to attract negativity. I just get up after a disaster day or time then think that I need good things and concentrate on what I want to achieve and work on that. When I receive an answer as NO, I would never get upset. No is always a new opportunity. So if it did not work now, something better is awaiting. Everything is about how you set your mind; thinking positive you will attract positive things. I am awake in the morning, looking at the window and then I thank God for another beautiful day in this world. Life is very precious by itself; we need to enjoy not to waste. Perfection does not exist and should never be expected. I am taking the best of the day and enjoying the time I am alive. Working long hours but really enjoying the job, enjoying the days off and making the most of them.

Next Friday, I am getting my own flat keys – really excited and incredibly happy. After seven months of nightmare from my ex-boyfriend, it worked out for the best... bought my own beautiful flat in a nice area. What more could I wish for! All my dreams came true... Brought up my son, gave him the best education; he's become a good human being; he also got brilliant job; I got a lovely job and beautiful flat. What could I ask more? Nothing. Just to thank God for His help to get to these days and enjoy every single day for the rest of my life!

And remember! Single is not a status; it is a word which describes a person who is strong enough to live and enjoy their life without depending on others!

During the years, I have experienced difficulties, disappointments from one or many more people and many unhappy moments. I never took anything as a complete disaster in my life. On the contrary, I have taken all as an experience of life which brings me out of my comfort zone. I am getting myself up constantly and reminding myself that these things are usual and are happening in life! I would most certainly learn from my mistakes, and I would become stronger, wiser and more experienced to deal with. I managed to put myself together after everything, and I look forward for my next goals, achievements and happiness in life. Learning step by step from mistakes, gave me the power for my future. Nothing would ever stop me until I climb towards the top of the stairs; I am incredibly determined! The power of the mind is keeping me going slowly day by day but surely step by step.

I never gave up on my goals and dreams during the years. I am happy I have managed to achieve many of them. Determination is the power which enables our capability to achieve everything in a life with a strong sense of motivation and commitment.

Chapter 18

I am now in my dream job, being an operation manager for events. As you can already imagine, every day is a different day and no two days are the same. The workplace, where I am currently working, has a massive park and a very traditional English country house. It is absolutely beautiful place, great for children interaction—has playgrounds—and family's countryside picnics. The house was built in 1490 and was originally a red-brick late Gothic manor house. The place is also known as a historic wild deer park. When I am driving to work, I am often welcomed by beautiful deer on the entrance, and this makes me so proud to be part of such fantastic place. Although technically my company is independent company subcontractor to this place, I feel a lot closer to it.

We are a team of approximately 9 people in the office plus all hospitality staff members. As I had travelled a lot in my past, I often felt like a visitor in every country I have been, even if I had already acquired citizenship. When I started to work here, I worked hard, with honesty and compassion to the best ability. I am a very open minded person and always happy to meet new people, and I was quite new in the area myself, I would have loved the team members to work together at work and be a strong team. We were so busy with events, especially with weddings, which I always felt as a big privilege to see a new couple having the best day of their life becoming reality through our company's help, doubling the satisfaction. We had not only successful days of work, but also made the newly married couples happy and joyful. I felt like my personality is very suitable for front line jobs, to work directly with people and to deal with all sorts of problems. To help with last minute requests by people smoothly, is something which I always enjoyed and found myself useful for. It takes a little effort for one to want to change something. I am working long hours because this is the type of work in hospitality, with many positive feedbacks which of course could make you proud of what you are doing. The beautiful room arrangements for wedding breakfast were one of the best aspects of my job which I really enjoyed taking responsibility for. Planning all the steps before the wedding is a job which I will never forget. Even after all my happy and hard-working moments at wok, unfortunately, I was never accepted by some of the team members; perhaps because of my strong personality as I always expressed myself with honesty and tried to explain that certain jobs could be done much easier if everyone liked what they were doing and were happy to help people not only because of their job, but also as a human being and took responsibility for each work task diligently. Obviously as I am not originally from England, I sometimes have strong accent, and further, I speak five other languages fluently, thus any person who is speaking different languages, naturally would have different accents. Because of the accent I have, I have been insulted and laughed at the most. Nevertheless, even after the difficulties, I never gave up on my job which I love. Pushing me away made me stronger and more dedicated to my work.

It was only the beginning of the week and I was doing some administration and planning jobs in the office, when suddenly, I had comment by one college from behind:

"Dora, if Brexit will happen and we get out of EU, then you will not be here anymore, remember this!"

I just laugh and replied:

"Darling, I still will be here, do not worry about me so much, I hold the same passport as you and on top of this, I have never been out of work and I am sure I will not be out of work or out of the country."

Everybody was shocked by our conversation, which showed how diversity of backgrounds was being expressed at work. I did not get offended, as it was not the first time when I had to deal with discrimination and will not be the last, I was sure. I just laughed and carried on with my work. I have never judged a single person by where they come form, I see people as human beings, and any factor such as: the skin colour, accent, or nationality, is completely irrelevant to me. I have had many ups and downs in my life. But I learned, before you judge the other person, just put yourself in their shoes and walk on their path, think within yourself "how would you manage to live in their situation?" A Single mum! Without any one of the family members! With no financial or moral support or help! When I had a discussion with my colleagues about it, the response was simple: I should not leave the country.

Chapter 19

Well!!!

If you are living daily life in domestic abuse and threatened to be killed, do you have an option?

No! Then, taking my life in my hands and travelling over the seas for mine and my child's safety was the only option I had as a single mother. As many who could have been through these things in life, we should remember we only become more honest and stronger people. I like to say the truth to people face to face, I do not like gossips or any sorts of office politics. That is why I was pushed away as I always was putting my cards on the table. However, I was happy that I was working on the front line with public, helping people, being there for them, which made me feel grateful every day.

It was a beautiful morning of May; I was again going to work as I was running two conferences today with another colleague. As always, with the smile on my face, I was preparing for the press conference which was to be held on that day at our working place. At about 10:30 in the morning, my sales manager, Leanne, came to me and asked:

"Dora, would you like to do some translation for one of the most famous Russian boxer, JU, in heavy league, who would be coming for the press conference but unfortunately his translator did not manage to arrive and they do not have any translator to be present now before the event starts shortly?"

This was a bit of surprise for me as I had not spoken Russian since I arrived in the UK from Israel, which were about 13 years. I requested:

"Well, I have not spoken Russian for the last 13 years, if they can give me an opportunity to speak with the boxer before the press conference, so I can make sure I can understand him, then I am more than happy to help them."

Leanne went back and explained to them that I can help just if I could speak before press conference with the boxer and check if we can understand each other. Leanne replied:

"Yes, they agreed to speak with you before the press conference as they do not have anyone else in this last-minute issue."

Always through my life I am so happy to help anybody no matter the cost as I know how important it is to be human in difficult moments. I think this is the reason why I was brought back from the clinical dead to express even more kindness, love for each other, respect for each other and help anyone on this earth. My faith in God is much stronger than anything on this earth. Whatever difficulties I face, I know they will pass and everything will get better. People often ask me about how I could smile after the things I have been through. We live only once on this earth, so never allow small grey moments to ruin your whole life; things come and go, but the time wasted in worries or regrets would never come back.

After an hour, I had the privilege to meet the Russian boxer, I spoke with him and his impresario. Surprisingly for me, I was understanding him well, just there was a bit of difficulty in replying back, however, I managed to brush out some forgotten parts before the conference started. At 12:00 midday, the press conference started, and I was next to him on the stage. Sitting next to him was a wonderful moment for me and not to mention there were many paparazzi and media companies surrounding us. It was an unusual experience! All the press conference run smoothly, they were happy with my translation and I was happy to help them and overall, I have had a wonderful experience. After the press conference, I showed them our working place and took them around for a walk in the deer's park. As I helped them in difficult moment with the translation, I have been rewarded with free VIP guest ticket to see the match. Me, my son, and his fiancée went to see the match, where the Russian boxer lost, unfortunately. These were wonderful experiences at work and later during the match, which I will never forget. I love the life when it is challenging, diverse and rewarding. After long day of work, we received particularly good feedback from the press conference organiser, and he thanked everyone on the team for the great help.

Going back to my daily job, as I mentioned it is hard hospitality driven job but extremely rewarding, every day is a different day, diverse people with various working style. This Saturday we had a wedding where the bride and her family were really concerned that they would not be on the standard request. It was Thursday, I had meeting with the bride, groom, and bride's parents for final details, I assured them that I will take care of everything and I will be with them during the whole time. If there would be any issue, just let me know. I promised them that they will have everything as they requested as it is special day for them, and it will be the perfect day.

Chapter 20

I asked them not to worry about the wedding night as I was on duty with my colleague, Marthy, and if anything, he will take care of everything that they request.

Friday morning, I was making sure that I had everything in place, ready for their special day as I took everything in my hands, and I would be responsible for their wedding. Saturday morning at 9 am, I was already at the venue to check everything to be ready. By lunch time, the bride and the groom arrived for their ceremony and I welcomed them. I told them to trust me with everything, just to enjoy the special day because it is a memorable day. I had everything under control. Everything went by the plan, wonderful wedding, everyone was happy, enjoying with no worries. Me and my colleague Marthy were happy as the wedding was going by the book. About 10 pm, I approached the bride's mother and asked her if everything was okay and if they needed anything else as I wanted to go home and leave my colleague, Marthy, to the end of the wedding as all the food was served, just drink and dance remained until everything ended.

She hugged me and the bride's dad and bride herself hugged me and said that they had a perfect, wonderful wedding day.

Everything was perfect! I went home, tired but with the smile on my face that I made many people happy on this special day and they will remember a perfect wedding day. Just wonderful when you can make other people happy and they appreciate you for that. After a couple of days, we received lovely feedback from this couple. Every day was different, exiting day at this job. I really appreciated the beautiful days which I could never forget.

It was such an unusual night I had. I could not fall asleep until late and finally when I managed to catch some sleep, I had such a weird dream that I remember till today. I was dreaming of livestock animals and cows surrounding me. I was very distressed and when I woke up I had a very strange feeling of worry. I spoke to my son and his fiancée in the morning and mentioned to them that I was feeling quite strange and worried as I had a dream last night which is very strange. I remembered from my grandparents that dreaming of such livestock and particularly cows was an indication of health danger. Nevertheless, I did not pay much attention to it and started the morning by preparing for work.

Again, Friday morning; I worked until late on previous day and had started earlier today as I had to meet the bride and groom for tomorrow's wedding. I checked all the details before they arrived. About 10:20 am, I was going to the meeting, passing by the park from my office to the meeting room; it was about 5 meters where I had to walk between office and events building. As I stepped outside the office, maybe few steps, I suddenly realised that my both legs had been caught in some rope or circle-shaped plastic, and I fell on my face on the gravelled stones. During the seconds in which I was falling on the ground, I realised I was falling on my face and then intuitively turned in a second on my side and put my hand forward to avoid my face. I felt pain on my arm, and I broke my elbow in many pieces. I lost consciousness for seconds, when I realised what have just happened. I said to my colleague from sales who was waking me up to call the ambulance because my elbow was gone, there was a hole in my elbow, blood was pouring from there as it was broken and I could not feel my arm at all. The shock was so high that I was not feeling the pain, however, I was shaking from stress.

After the ambulance took me, the doctor confirmed that the hand was broken, and I needed operation on my elbow as it was broken from many places and needed to be reconstructed as a whole new elbow. Also, it would be needed to put a metal plate in the elbow to keep all pieces together. As it was Friday, also I was allergic to metal, they needed to find titanium plate as alternative so they said operation would take place tomorrow, on Saturday. They wrapped the hand for now in plaster cast. The pain started to be horrible, so I was given morphine, which is one of the strongest pain reliefs given during medical conditions. Meanwhile, my son with his fiancée, arrived to see me in the hospital, brought me clothes to change, his fiancée helped me to wash myself as with one hand it is terribly hard. They stayed until late with me. On Saturday early morning, the doctor said not to eat anything as I would be admitted in the theatre for surgery later on. They found a titanium plate and were ready to take me for surgery. I was admitted at 12 noon, with originally planned time of one and a half hour surgery, but the operation took more than 3.5 hours, as they reconstructed my elbow completely to give it a new shape; surgeons had to put 6 screws on the sides and one across to keep every piece together. I came back from anaesthesia about 5 pm. My kids were worrying that I was not waking up.

Since day one after the operation, I have always complained about the shoulder pain. The doctors sent me home one day after the operation as they had completed the check on me. Being under morphine, I was feeling bearable, but when I got home and started to take painkillers, I felt terrible pain in my shoulder. I returned to hospital on the 3rd day as it was unbearable pain. Hospital was checking the elbow which was operated not the shoulder where I was saying that I feel this terrible pain. They changed my painkillers and sent me back home. Since then, I had to deal days and nights with terrible pain. At nights, if I managed to sleep 2 uninterrupted hours, it felt like a lot to me, the rest of the night I walked around the flat in order to engage my brain to stop focusing on the pain.

After the first weeks, as pain was unbearable, I had my full arm wrapped in plaster cast for few weeks, and all the x-rays showed my collarbone was damaged as well. The pain was spread across the shoulder and the arm. First few days after injury I was fairly sure that in 5-6 weeks I will recover and will be back to work. Unfortunately, my plans did not work accordingly. During the injury, I did not only had the elbows broken but also collarbone was affected and now the shoulder. The bone connecting the shoulder to the elbow was not recovering as quick as it was expected to. After 6 weeks, I started physiotherapy for elbows, unfortunately the shoulder pain restricted a lot of the movements I could do. The fracture of the elbows caused other issues at the same time, such as the muscle problems, as the rotator cuff muscles had been damaged, which was very painful. Elbow fracture is extremely painful itself plus shoulder pain, you could imagine the severe pain I was going through and none of the regular painkiller prescribed were managing to help with the pain. After 6 weeks, the plaster cast was removed, then I only had a sling to hold the arm and to try to control the pain with reduced movement. During this time, I attended many of the A & E for help. Plus, all the consultant appointments. The recovery was terribly slow with a lot of pain. If someone was able to tell me what I will have to suffer from single fall on the ground I would not have believed. It was the second month after the injury occurred, I was still with my arm in a sling, attending physio but everything was just not going as expected. The usual housework of cooking, taking care of myself such as basic wash my hair was extremely hard with one hand, still relied on my future daughter in law to come over the weekend and help me. The elbow was more manageable now, however, the shoulder pain was not improving at all. I kept changing medication but with no luck to be pain free. I was trying everything as I was determined to sort out this pain forever, however, it did not seem to be in my power. I had been told by the consultant that these problems with shoulder and elbows together could take up to 18 months. I was completely speechless after that, to my surprise, I asked to clarify if he meant 18 weeks.

"No, up to 18 months could take to recover." the consultant confirmed.

However, as I did not have many options at the moment, one thing I tried with all my ability was to get away from the pain so I could have some sleep at night.

On 31 September I had another appointment with the consultant, and I was looking forward to finding the cause of this pain, simply I could not carry on with the same pain. During the consultation as usual, the doctor was concentrated on the elbow as that was the focal point for surgery, but the shoulder was not being taken into much account. The consultant said, "Everything is looking good on the elbows and you can go home." I started to cry straightaway and said, "I cannot bear this pain anymore and I will not go home until the pain is not dealt with!" The consultant got slightly upset but I said that even if now I received injection which could help ease the pain, it would not explain the reason of the pain and how it was to be permanently dealt with? I am a single person; I have to pay my mortgage and I want to go back to work, I do not want to stay indoors and take painkillers constantly. During this discussion, the consultant decided to give me an injection in my shoulder at the same time at least to try to help somehow to recover after 3 months spent indoors most of the time. Still restricted from driving, confined to indoors, at least I got some help from my friends Bella, Oly, Marthy and Jane to do some shopping and get me out a bit from the house after 3 months of being locked.

During this 3-month period, I learned that sometimes as human beings we are tested to see how we can cope with difficulties and struggles especially if we are alone. With all the struggle, pain, lack of sleep, I was still optimistic that the time will come when I will get back on my feet myself again. I was grateful to God every day that I was alive, I had roof over my head, food on the table, electricity, heating in my flat, program on the TV any time, connection to the internet to connect with the world. Nowadays very few of us acknowledge these things as blessings, as they are perceived as basics. If I had to give any advice to anybody, I would definitely say that if you have access to these facilities in your homes and you are healthy, be grateful for everything. I lived life under a lot of restrictions as well, under domestic abuse, under threats for my life which is completely different life from what we live these days.

After another 4 weeks, I had another injection which helped me to recover slowly but steadily. Really I was looking forward to going back to work. Slowly started to drive to get the confidence with my arm as it was still painful when I was using it to drive, but slowly, after short distance I was getting on the road. Luckily, the workplace was not far away so I started to drive to work. I did return to work, my recovering was still far away from being pain free, however, I continued physio, waiting for another ultrasound-guided subacromial injection to be done as last MIR showed that I had some subacromial bursitis and attenuated long head of biceps. Starting to work was helping me to get over quicker as I was in contact with people every day. Enjoying simple things as sunrise, sunset of the day can make you happy living on this earth, appreciating little things will put smile on your face.

Chapter 21

With all these ups and downs, I still managed to finish level 2 accountancy. I remember when I appeared on the sitting exams with arm fully plastered, invigilators asked me:

"How are you going to manage to do the exam with one hand?"

"I will manage, I do not want to delay any of the exams which I had booked previously."

I wanted to sit the exams the dates which were booked and for everybody's surprise I was the oldest student with plastered arm on the exam day and I scored the highest result (85% to 92%) on all exams. This is a great proof of how determination for achievement could be achieved if you just have ambition. Towards my struggling with pain, lack of sleep and stress, I carried on with everything that I had planned before, I did not allow to lose any of the time because of the broken arm. I am still dealing with pain these days as it is an ongoing process. I have already started level 3 of accountancy and I have booked my two further exams as I really do not like to lose the time for doing nothing. Time is precious, we are on a transit life, using time, enjoying, or losing the feeling of being sorry for ourselves. We have this one opportunity in our own hands that depends on which pathway we decide to walk, a happy pathway or a miserable pathway. I am an optimist for everything and I am always looking for happy days from any enjoyment; walking in the park with my friends, or have nice chat on the phone with friends or relatives, family – things which we should enjoy and be grateful. If we are looking world around at much wider level, some countries are having a real struggle, people are living in camps, fighting for daily safety, living from food donations; some people do not have the "luxury life" which we call basic nowadays and I can see they still are happy to be alive and survive every day. My mother always said to live a life with clean soul, help people who need your help because we do not know how long we will be in this transit life on Earth. It is given to us to live wisely. Whenever you do things, do not rush through life. Rushing through life will bring you stress and unhappiness, that is why it is important to work to live but not live to work.

I always try to find ideas which make me happy, try new experiences, find myself and appreciate. If you like to study anything and improve yourself, do it, it is never too late and remember you are never too old for anything as long as you want it. Everything is in our hands; I really enjoy sometimes just driving and admire the beauty of nature around us. Do not let the time slip away from us! I can see myself how time is going day by day and I know time would come where we would ask ourselves, how many of my dreams I have managed to fulfil, and did I try at all? Until today, I can say for myself that most of my dreams did indeed come true. Some of them I worked awfully hard to accomplish, and I know I would not give up until I achieve them.

Chapter 22

Last year in the late autumn, I received a surprising phone call from my old friend Jacob from Israel, we used to work in the same place during the time when I worked there. We did not see each other for about 5 years, last time we met was when I went on holiday in Israel. Jacob called me to say that he is coming to visit London and if I am free to meet up for a dinner and to go around with him. We used to go for evening classes to dance Salsa. I was so happy to hear that he was coming to visit London. I took few days off work as he was coming alone for the first time and would have been nice to show him around. He booked 10 days to visit UK. I was happy to see him, so I offered to pick him up from the airport and took him to the hotel in London where he had his booking. It was Tuesday afternoon, I picked up Jacob from the airport, then we walked to the car to drive to the hotel. We went to the hotel, parked in the hotel parking, and just went to the reception so he could check in. He dropped his luggage, changed and then we went around the city. I knew London better, I used to live there, he said that he would be happy if I took him just around the city. His hotel was in Euston, we walked down to the Strand, I showed him the beautiful theatres there as I had booked a ticket for us to go to see

"Mama Mia" show. Jacob loved every place we were walking around, the architecture on the buildings around as well. From there, we walked down to the Waterloo bridge where he can see the London Eye. Walking together, we were talking about our lives and how everything had turned out, what we did in these years and how was everything back there in Israel as well. He was amazed by the amount of people in the rush hour in central London. He was living in Tel-Aviv and he said that his city was busy but seeing the amount of people in London after work was impressive, just the capacity of London city in centre. As the night was falling, we went to the restaurant to have a dinner. Often, when we are visiting another country for the first time, traditional food is the best option in order to gain some more flavour and taste of the local culture. I recommended lovely steak and chips plus he had time to try something new every day. During the dinner he asked me:

"Dora, could you tell me a bit about London, you are living here for many years, so tell me how has the City captured you to stay for so long, what is so fascinating about London?"

I laughed and said that I do not know a lot, but I remember some since I studied the British history before I was awarded with British citizenship.

"Well, London was founded by the Romans 1000-1100 B.C. and has thrived over the centuries. I know London is quite rich in history, with legendary kings. I remember by the third century it was Londinium, the name given by Romans. As you know London is one of the most significant financial and cultural capital cities in the world. London was attacked many times the same as Israel had terrorist attacks during the years. I will take you to see Tower of London, we will take a ride on River Thames. One interesting thing is that in London over 300 languages are spoken. As we will go along the places, I will tell you little stories I know about the individual places. I planned for you to go visit many places as I am off this week as well."

We had nice dinner then I took him back to the hotel in Euston where he stayed, and I went back to my flat. I drove back, when I got home Jacob called me and said that he is so excited about his trip that could not even catch a sleep. We still had a long chat then I said good night and that I will come to London by train to avoid the parking issues. Wednesday morning, I caught the train to London and went to meet Jacob in his hotel. I had many surprises for him which I was sure he would never forget about during this trip. We started the day with a lovely coffee in one of the coffee shops in Holborn, then we caught one of the famous touristic buses to Westminster. We went to see Big Ben, just from outside as we did not book a visit inside. Walking around, we paid tribute to PC Keith Palmer who was so unfortunately killed in a terror attack, I told him how PC and 4 pedestrians have been killed in the terror attack by Khalid Masood. PC Palmer died on his duty and deserves all tribute that could be given. Jacob understood as in Israel they often face very similar situations. From there, we went to London Eye where I had the surprise tickets to go on.

London Eye, standing 135m tall on the South Bank of the River Thames. Since the 2000s, it opened the doors to millions of people coming to visit this beautiful place. Jacob was admiring the beauty of the site, and adored every beauty of London from 135m above. After the tower on London Eye, he said he could not believe that it would be so beautiful to even take pictures from there, if someone would be telling him, he would not have believed. He said himself, he will recommend to his friends to go on such a trip and visit the old London. We walked down to the South Bank by the River Thames to show him the beautiful statue and sculptures, also the street performers on south bank London such as Charlie Chaplin which was performing on that day. It was a special place for tourists who were coming for the first time. Me and Jacob started to talk about everything like we knew each other our entire lives. It was remarkably interesting how comfortable we were in each other's company and how happy we were to spend time together. After long day of walking, we were feeling a bit tired, so we decided to go to have dinner at the place where he was staying. Also, I did not have to walk far away to go to underground station. Dinner was amazing, the interesting fact was that he had asked for kosher dinner at the hotel and they said that they had kosher food in their kitchen as well. Jacob really enjoyed everything that he was experiencing. I said:

"Jacob, I have a surprise for you for tomorrow, we will go to the theatre to see show called, Mama Mia!"

"You are a star Dora, you are looking after me so good, I would not have managed to see all these places by myself. I really appreciate you took off work to spend time with me and take me around."

I was happy to hear lovely appreciation. I replied:

"That is what friends are for, you were nice to me when I was in Israel and now is my turn to be nice to you and show you around in London."

Then we had just lovely chat again about the time spent together back in Israel. Those were days I would never forget, the memorable time and places at which we stayed, will be with me forever. Every place has its beauty, I was amazed by Israelites' culture myself, in all respect of the current problems known in Israel, people and places make the memorable time then the political state of the country. Every country has positive and negative things that is why we should never be looking for negatives but instead, we should be looking for positive things. It was time for me to get on the way home, when you spend time with someone you like, time flies by and then there is only enough time to remember all the memories. We arranged to meet next day afternoon as we felt a bit tired and I left Jacob to do some shopping in the morning, then we were going to see the Tower Bridge and Tower of London then we would get ready in the hotel to go to theatre. When we got to the Tower of London, I told him that the castle is 900 years old and has served many purposes: royal residence, barracks, armoury, prison, and museum. Also, it had many famous and infamous prisoners there. The Tower was designated as a World Heritage site by UNESCO. Tower of London is a historic castle alongside the north bank of the River Thames in central London. Walking across Tower Bridge, Jacob asked me if I knew when it was built as it looked more historic.

"Jacob, I am not sure exactly in which year it was built but what I remember is that it would have been built between 1886 and 1894, this Bridge crosses the River Thames close to the Tower of London. I came few times to visit here with my relatives and they asked me the same question, luckily, I started studying British history then I remembered some of it."

We went to the hotel, changed for the evening, had something to eat and we went to see "Mama Mia" at Novello Theatre in Strand, London. Theatre is beautiful, we found our seats in the middle rows, we left our coats on the chairs and Jacob said he wanted to stop by the drink bar before the show starts. We went to the bar, got our drinks, and really enjoyed the lovely show. The music, the arrangement of Greek Island's paradise combined together were fabulous. Since then, I watched the show again few times more. Jacob said after this amazing show we needed to have a nice dinner as well. We went to the Indigo Restaurant, and Jacob said he wanted to formally thank me for all the tours I had taken him on and he said he never felt so happy and he never enjoyed someone's company the way he was enjoying with me these days. He mentioned that it was something special which brought him to London. We both loved each other's company, but we never had an open discussion if we would like to have more than a friend relationship. Being both single for many years, we had realised how happy we were in company of each other and only after so many years knowing each other we were opening discussion about ourselves. We ended up until late in the restaurant without realising that the time was flying by. Walking to the hotel slowly, we found it romantic, feeling like we were younger again. Whenever there is a sparkle of love, the age is just a number? Love does not have age; every person has heart and if there is love in the heart, it could be in their older age and would still be the same and magical.

I think we found each other's love which we were both looking for years elsewhere. I stayed in the hotel with Jacob, we talked until early morning about our lives, work, and possible future together. On the next day we woke up next to each other with the smile on our faces and realised after so many years knowing each other, we found the happiness together.

Yet another day, we visited British Museum, National Gallery, The Shard and Buckingham Palace. The day was amazing around the London. I still enjoyed visiting all these places in London, I had already seen them many times, but I still loved visiting them. Jacob was amazed by all these places as well and was already thinking ahead to book another holiday with the family. We were spending quality time together visiting beautiful places. We were remembering our time in Israel, all our friendship for many years. We were taking our time to enjoy every moment together. Jacob wanted to see where I lived so I decided to take him to my place to show him some places out of London.

This evening, we took the train to my place. He was excited to have the opportunity to visit many places. Spending the evening with him, with a lovely home cooked dinner; salmon with new potato and green beans. Life is so good when you have someone who understands you and makes you laugh. At certain age, all you need is companionship, to have someone to chat, this is what makes you happy. The next day was his last day in London, we were going to Cambridge to see Cambridge university, and other historical places. The time was going so quickly, like yesterday, I was looking forward for Jacob to finally arrive. It was so sad that he had to leave; however, we started our relationship and we were looking forward for next lovely holiday to book together. After we spent the day together in Cambridge, we planned our holiday to Australia in January 2019.

Jacob returned safely to Israel, incredibly happy about his experience in London, and our relationship. What an amazing week we had together!

Developing a very close relationship to an old friend is such a good feeling, especially at this age. Relaxed after a week of holiday and traveling together, I was happy to come back to work. We started talking every evening on the phone and looked forward for our planned holiday. We booked the tickets already, for Australia. Now we were planning the places we wanted to visit and the trip to this far place. I had been there before, but Jacob never had the chance to visit. Meanwhile in November, I was flying to Israel to see him and plan our itinerary. He had beautiful house in Tel-Aviv, with lovely garden, not far away from the seaside. We went for a walk by the seaside, I loved the alleyway with palmier on both sides, the happiness on the people's faces makes you happy in a way that you are part of this lively place. I admire the people's attitude in Israel, they have experienced so many things there, but they have always remained happy, probably the climate influences this as well, warmth and sunshine most of the time could be making people happier.

Spending the long weekend with Jacob, we were both looking forward to our next trip to spend holiday together. He took me to Jerusalem, to the old city and my favourite place. We spent a bit of time in the church and I went to the chapel where Jesus is buried, place where I always find the peace in my soul. Jerusalem is a city that many people say makes them frightened because you could see many armed soldiers on the streets, I was feeling more secure seeing the police on the street, maybe because I lived for good many years in Israel. From the old city, Jacob said we should go to the Western

Wall (knowing as Wailing Wall or HaKotel) a place of prayer and pilgrimage for the Jewish people but also for others who believe. Approximately 1.5 million of the people there were foreign tourists. As we walked, there were so many people praying, it is a special place where people from all over the world come for the same reason, to pray to God. Finding love, happiness, and respect between two people from different countries is remarkably interesting, we had similar interests, I spoke fluent Hebrew, this was an advantage for me to have common language. Jacob was always amazed how I had strong determination to learn the language as there are people who are still living in Israel for many years and they do not speak the language. Also I found it interesting as a language, probably, to be able to learn so quickly; however, I always wanted to know the language of the country where I was in for a while. If it would be possible to learn, it was a plus for me.

Chapter 23

"Dora darling, would you like a surprise?"

"Yes love, only if it would be nice surprise!"

"I am sure you would love it, as I remember from many years ago. this was a special place for you."

"Hope it is not too far as on Tuesday morning I am flying back to the UK."

"No, tomorrow we will go to Haifa, to Bahai Gardens, if you would like, I will drive you there."

"Yes, definitely. Thank you, I am off as well, so I would love to go with you to Haifa."

I was so excited to see these places again for their historical significance and natural beauty. On Monday morning, we drove to Haifa, it took us about one hour and ten minutes. Jacob parked in the central parking then we walked around. We walked alongside, then Jacob asked me:

"Darling do you know the original name of the Bahais Garden?"

"No, I know just that it is called Bahais Garden."

"The original name is: Shrine of the Bab."

"Why, what is the story behind, I know there must be a story behind?"

"The name was coming from the founder on the Babi Faith who died and had been buried in the Baha I Faith in 1909. His remains were buried in a six-room mausoleum made out of local stones."

"Jacob who is Baha?"

"The Bahai Faith is a religion, teaching the essential worth of all religions, and the unity of all people. Placed in Persia and Middle East, and it's known as second holiest place in the world. The garden is a combination of Western and Persian style. The plants were brought from all over the world symbolising the unity of God and humans. There are 1,200 steps from the German Colony at the foot on the terraces to the lockout at the top."

"That is interesting, I remember that there were 1,200 steps because I went once up the dome by steps. But I did not know what the terraces symbol is as they were quite few."

"Darling, there are 19 perfectly arranged terraces descending from Mount Carmel to the German Colony. On the Bahai calendar there are 19 months, each of which has 19 days. Because 19 times 19 is 361, they celebrate their New Year on March 21, the Equinox. Whenever the day equal the night in terms of hours, the 4 days that are not counted in the calendar, this is the reason why we have 365 days and they have 361 days in a calendar."

"Wow, thank you my love, if you were not bringing me here today, I would have never learned all this new interesting history. Wow really appreciate this visit!"

As we were approaching the Dome, Jacob just reminded me that we had to take off our shoes on the entrance.

"If you remember, Dora?"

"Yes, of course, I remember that."

Standing on the top next to the Dome and looking down was beautiful, I am sure whoever was visiting will never forget this place. It was such a unique place; I visited many countries, but I had never seen anywhere such magnificent and impressive garden architecture.

"Jacob, the history I learned today, I will remember throughout my whole life. Thank you for bringing me here."

"I knew that you would love it. I know you." Jacob replied.

"Now, are we going to have some grilled fish from the sea on a Haifa port, there was a restaurant which prepares fresh fish?"

"Yes, darling, that sounds very good."

We had exceptionally good dinner, on the seaside before we headed to Tel-Aviv back. I spent long wonderful weekend in Israel. I was flying back and making good time as I still had 20 min from Jacob's house to Tel-Aviv airport, flight is four hours, and 20 minutes from London airport to my flat. Very easy and straight forward journey. We continued to keep close contact, calling each other in the evening as technology is so advanced nowadays, we were able to see each other on skype as well.

All the planning for Australia was done, now few months to work, I had quite busy days before the long journey, which is usually done once in a lifetime. I was lucky to go for second time, because of my new love who wanted me to go and was taking me with him. It was so much easy for us to go on together, probably because we knew each other for many years, we worked in the same building, been friends, we also knew a lot about each other's lives. Knowing the person for so many years makes it much easier to trust the person, otherwise I would have been worrying to travel with someone from so far away whom I cannot trust. The best was that Jacob was coming to England few days before we were traveling, and we were able to leave together.

January the 20th, pouring dawn as we are preparing for our journey. Jacob was double checking and asking second time.

"Dora, what time is the taxi coming tomorrow morning?"

"Darling our flight is at 12:10 noon, taxi is book for 8:00 am to Heathrow so we can have time to get there and not rush to check in, but instead, have a coffee before, so I think that will work, what do you think? Would you like earlier or you think this is OK?"

"That's perfect, Dora, it's perfect time."

We were overly excited for this trip; I knew that it will be unforgettable holiday. In the morning, I just heard the voice of Jacob as I was still in a bed.

"Dora, as it is not raining, we got a perfect day to get to the airport."

His excitement and happiness in his voice sounded so lovely. He came back kissed me; he was so happy that we were going together on this trip. Taxi arrived at 7:50 am, we were ready for traveling. When you travel with someone compatible, it is so much easier with everything, we were agreeing so easily on the things which we both loved and wanted to experience. It was already a good journey, in 40 minutes, we got to the airport. Having a lot of time gave us the opportunity to explore the Heathrow airport as well, being so big it is busy all the time. We had interchange in Hong Kong for 6 hours, then we had another flight to Australia. As we embarked on the flight, the feelings were so special for having Jacob with me, after 6 months of corresponding with him, spending some time with him; this trip was about to prove if it was going to work with our distance relationship and if we were matching each other. We had a nice meal on the flight, drinks as well, chatting and watching movie, we realised that we will be in Hong Kong in an hour. I had never been at this airport, so I was excited to see the new place in the new country. We landed in Hong Kong and were directed to the waiting area. We decided to walk around first to see the shops, the airport, and then we will come back to the waiting area. Every place was unique on its own, the arrangements, the culture. People were so polite, helpful, and we were being asked by many staff members if we needed any help with anything, if we knew where we were going, which shops we were looking for. Amazing people admire them for their hospitality. I would really recommend visiting to see how friendly and polite people are. Flight crew was with the same polite and friendly attitude, respectful and helpful. I really appreciated and it made me happy that there are people with good hearts despite difference in culture, religion, or nationality. After two hours of walking around, we had time to rest in a coffee area for 2 hours until we embarked on the flight to Australia. While relaxing and resting in the waiting room, we heard announcement which was reminding for the check in for next flight to Australia. Jacob and I were ready to go in a second, I said:

"Darling, do not panic, we got plenty of time."

He just smiled and said that his adrenaline of traveling was high, he always had when he was traveling, he was a bit worried and scared, as soon as we would arrive and land on the destination, the adrenaline will fall down. We laughed together. We were on the flight to Australia; we settled well;

we had been offered meal then we went to sleep. They started to serve the meals already and we had two meals plus snack. We were really spoiled with food from different varieties. We enjoyed the dinner, with drinks and we had a sleep as we still had about nine hours to fly. After good hours of sleep, I found Jacob watching me as he could not fall asleep then did not wanted to disturb me, was just quietly watching me. When I opened my eyes, he smiled and said that he was looking after me and I could sleep more. As I woke up, we put on a movie to watch as everyone was sleeping or watching something but was so quiet in the flight that you really could relax. The last meal was served before we landed to Australia. I tried different food and really enjoyed the long flight.

As we arrived at the Sydney airport, we have checked in the hotel, it was sunny day as it was the summer here, we were looking forward to our first adventure to the Sydney Harbour Bridge. As we had arrived during lunch time, we went for walk in Sydney to see around the interesting bridges built over the water and we booked a traditional bus trip at night in Sydney. Jacob was so happy; you can see his face was radiating the joy. I was admiring his excitement alongside the wonderful places we were visiting. The bus tours were booked, and we were really looking forward to it. We went to hotel after a while as it was quite hot, we had a rest and went for a walk later on. Having a big difference in time zones of UK, Israel, and Australia, we felt this tiredness and decided just to stay and rest. We slept in the flight, however, as you can image it could never be the same quality of sleep. We had a good rest and sleep to be ready for the next day as we had planned to go to Sydney. We woke up in arms of each other, smiling and getting ready for the new adventure. We had breakfast and coffee in the hotel and went to the Sydney Harbour Bridge to climb as we had booked for 10 am. We got there, and were welcomed by the crew, they explained how it worked and all the safety procedures. We had to wear special jumpsuit for this, and we were tied to the metal so that we do not fall from the bridge. We were a group of 6, plus a guide tour. The Sydney Harbour Bridge stands 135 metres above the water. The roadway is 51 metres above the sea level. Everyone had a radio with microphone in order to communicate among us. When walking so high, you can get a bit of head spinning, one of the reasons why everyone needs to be careful and walk slowly and safely. The tour guide explained that the original bridge was opened in 1932. It spans about 500 metres and is the longest steel-arch bridge in the world. When we got to the top and stopped to look down, the cars and people seemed so small. The view of Sydney looked stunning. Sydney opera house seemed beautifully designed from top of the bridge. Time was going so fast. Jacob was over the moon to see these places. He kept saying if I had not come with him, he would never had seen it.

"I am delighted to accompany you; I am so excited to be with you and experience this holiday together."

We ended the day with a dinner on a boat around Sydney with delicious food and music, which left beautiful memories. The weeks passed so quickly in Sydney, we visited Lone Pine Park. We flew to Great barrier reef and enjoyed every moment together. From there, we went to Melbourne. We went to find out more about the history of Australia.

This experience as I have already said is once in a lifetime and I am very thankful to God for it. We walked down the harbour, hand in hand, like in the movies. Love does not have age! When would I have imagined that after everything in my life, I would be that happy, surrounded by love, family, and new adventures. If I would have given up long time ago, I would have never had the chance to taste this sweet and wonderful piece of life. It is worth it, always fight for your life because all of us deserve the right of freedom and happiness and enjoy it. I have been extra lucky to be with someone who really takes care of me all the time. Thank you, Jacob, and looking forward to our life together.

CPSIA information can be obtained
at www.ICGtesting.com
Printed in the USA
LVHW040926290322
714698LV00014B/712